THE BREATH OF EUROPE

KIRYOWA IDRISA

Made with ♥ on the Notion Press Platform
www.notionpress.com

I would like to dedicate this book to the following people:

Mother: You are the reason for all my journeys in life, and no matter what I go through, I will never forget your words of wisdom. I have no anyone who has, will, and loves me the way you do. I love you so much, and I will always treasure you, for you are my beginning of life and your guidance and nurture are paramount. Whatever wrongs I do, challenges I face, and successes I reach are all because you are always supportive and prayerful for me.

Aunt: Among superwomen, you are the leader of all. With all the encouragement and all the friendship, we share besides mother and son. You are the best reason for all the tours I make worldwide. "Life is as you make it" will always be in my head because it keeps me positive and persistent. I can not thank you enough, but I can only be grateful because I have you as a mother, aunt, and best friend.

Dr. R. Pappu: From having me as an intern to supporting me as a mentor, you are worth a thousand things in all people's life. When the journey seemed impossible, you were the reason why I got "Hope" that I was praying from God. All the narrations in this book are because of your trust and encouragement, from financial support to processing, and I will always treasure your services to me as a student and as a person under your guidance.

Thank you, all.

Contents

Contents

Preface

A young African man in his middle 20s studying in India at Gitam University, K.Idrisa had gotten an amusing and amazing opportunity in his life of setting a foot in Europe a region comprising 27 countries, all with free movement, trade, etc., across all borders. This region is hope for most people from Africa and Asia, with a few from the American areas. This was too big to dream of, but suddenly it came true. It has always been his desire and passion to travel, but because Europe was hardcore, he had never hoped to travel there.In the last weeks of June 2022, he received a scholarship offer for a summer school program, "Sustain MV," which invited him to Germany. To him, this was music to his ears, as he claims to have applied for many summer school programs in Europe but received many rejections. Germany was the song to sing at that time.The story of his journey to Europe was full of surprises and exciting things right from when he got the scholarship offer to the time of going and back.The process was not as easy as everyone would predict, it was full of up and downs because getting a European visa is not a piece of cake, and being a holder of an African passport, he had to get a visa ("an access") to Europe. Amidst all the challenges that he went through, he got all the required documents and processed the visa, and went to Europe. He arrived in Poland (Warsaw), then a long layover to Germany (Berlin) to finally Greifswald. Having reached to final destination, he had to commence with the summer program had brought him. The program was from 22nd August to 2nd September, 2022. He attended all the program schedules and many other things which he enjoyed in Germany, including museums, markets, theatres, local clubs, churches, and different cities and states in Germany.

Foreword

Part of my Group at Sustain MV

Acknowledgements

I would like to acknowlwdge the following persons and institutions.

Naiga Amina, for keeping me motivated all the time and encouraging me to keep moving. •

S. Vidya for all the support you gave me and your family, I am grateful. This book would not have been written without your support.

GITAM University for supporting me in the process of writing the book, proofreading and directing me to the publication press.

Notion Press Platform who have allowed me publish my book as a starter writer at no cost so as to express my writing passion and message to the world.

CHAPTER ONE

Introduction

I love traveling, and it's my passion and my hobby. I always search the internet and look for opportunities requiring me to travel to different countries. A good example is about the trip I made to Egypt, which I wrote in my book, "The Egypt Boy," which I got from the internet when I searched for leadership conferences that were fully funded. One more thing I always give attention to is the emails that come to my emails which involve travels like conferences, summits, summer exchange programs, and summer schools. This trip was not so memorable in the sense that I got like other usual means. I can't explain how everything started, but the little I recall was opening my email in the morning, as it is my routine an,d seeing the call for application from the Sustain MV group. This email was sent through my college on our college mail IDs. The mail was as below.

Dear GITAM Student,

This is to inform you that a GITAM partner university in Germany is inviting applications for fully funded on-site summer school in mid-August. Students of Bachelor, Master, and Ph.D. students in any sustainability-related subject area can apply. Application Forms are open NOW: Registration link. SustainMV is jointly organized by the Higher Education Institutions of Mecklenburg- Western Pomerania. The goal is to present northeast Germany as the fantastic location for sustainability education, research, and business that it is. The on-site summer school is preceded by an online part which is highly recommended to attend for all on-site students. The application will be open until June 1ˢᵗ. A final decision concerning the scholarship holders can be expected in mid-June.

For detailed information, please see the attached fact sheet or visit our website https:// sustainmv.de/

Contact Carmen Opolski and Elisabeth Reich to answer any questions and concerns: info@sustainmv.de

GITAM International Affairs Office

This made me confirm that this was legit, so I had to apply. I always share such emails with my friends because they usually don't open their student emails, as most of the emails sent from the university are reminders. I went through the mail and hovered over the website where the whole information about the summer school, application procedure, and the deadline for application were displayed. Little did I know that I had once applied to the same summer school for 2021, but due to COVID-19, it was scheduled online. Having a clear picture and the required information, I started the application process by collecting the required documents and setting myself up for the application. One thing I can not forget is that the International Students' Office shared this opportunity, so I had to contact the office and get to know more about the hosting universities and the relationship between them and our university. I had to do it that day. If I remember well, the deadline was five days after seeing the application call. The reality is that I don't like doing things at the last minute, so I had to complete the application two days before the application deadline.

Application

I will be brief with the application process because not everyone wants to hear what is asked in the application and what were my responses. I collected all the required documents, i.e., Student ID, Passport, Confirmation of admission, motivational script, and references which all took me around two days to gather. I rushed to apply. In no more than 6 hours, I was done with the application, and I submitted just on time to my " before two days" plan. What I can't forget from the application process was the question: What motivated you to gain interest in the Sustain MV summer school program 2022? (word limit, 500). I never had an answer to this question. Still, I remember that in the year 2021, I attended the online session, and they had a lot of fascinating topics about sustainability, science, technology, culture, and diversity with tourism inclusive. I went to the website and checked the program outline because it was laid down clearly. The program had topics like Using light to do chemistry, Sustainable Tourist, Renewable energy and Hydrogen, Tours in different cities in Germany, and Cultural activities, this brought me motivation and interest, and as I wrote my interests, the 500-word limit was less. The biggest motivation was the fact that I have a passion for sustainable development and green Energy and technology, so when I saw many of the topics falling into that category, I got enthusiastic and eager to know more about sustainable developments in Germany and Europe at large.

Waiting time

After the application, I rested everything in the hands of the Lord. I kept praying every day for my application to be selected among the many. I had got many rejected applications for exchange programs and summer schools. I applied in different countries like China, South Korea, Japan, and UAE, but all I was getting is Rejection. My prayers increased day by day, with constant checking of my email. Since I had rejections from Asian countries, which I was studying in India, an Asian country, my hopes for the Germany Summer school Scholarship was in the hands of God. It took like one month and a half when I was not getting any email from the Sustain MV committee. I waited till the announcement time, and I checked my email again. I was broken because I had not gotten any email about an Offer or Rejection. I waited for the next day and nothing. At that time, I knew I was rejected, and I had to let go. After a few days, by that time, we were in the month of June. I decided to check on the organization's website, and that's when I saw the social media handles, I perused through them to get Updates, but I saw nothing, as the latest news was three months back. During this time, I was almost at the end of my semester(IV) and soon getting prepared for End of semester exams. I kept having this stress on my head and checking my email but nothing. One day I decided to email the sustain MV committee because they had given the contact information on their website. I decide to email because it is expensive to call in Germany from India. The mail read;

Greetings, sir/madam,

I am K. Idrisa, a student of Biotechnology at Gitam University India, I hear by writing to request information regarding the Sustain MV summer school to which I applied and expected to get feedback a few days back, but I have not gotten feedback yet. I will be glad to hear from you.

Thank you.

Regards,

K.Idrisa.

After sending the mail, I waited the whole day for a reply, but all was in vain. So I calmed myself down and said to my heart that if I were to be part of this program, I would receive the mail no matter what and if I was not to be part, even if I sent 100 mails. So I chilled and lowered my stress.

Scholarship Offer

The next day, I got a reply, and I was selected for the scholarship, but they never gave an explanation as to why I never got the email. Though at that moment, that was not an important issue, so I was so happy and even called my Aunt; she is my best friend and my mother beside my biological mother. She was the happiest. At that time, the mail of the scholarship offer was so wordy and long, but there was a note that stated, **"Your scholarship covers accommodation in full, meals and transport."** the rest did not matter at that time. The email read:

Dear Idrisa,

First of all, thank you very much for applying for SustainMV 2022 on-site. We received a lot of applications and would like to inform you that based on your application, you were selected for a scholarship

CONGRATULATIONS!

Please let us know as soon as possible, but at the latest, until Friday, July 1st, if you accept the scholarship offer for SustainMV on-site from August 22nd until September 1st. Please also remember that the online part of SustainMV 2022, taking place from August 15th until August 18th, is strongly recommended for on-site students.

In the following, please find some helpful information concerning the next steps. You will receive a piece of detailed pre-departure information about a month before the beginning of Summer School.

Visa

Do you need a visa invitation? Check the information on the webpage of the Federal Foreign Office: https:// www.auswaertiges-amt.de/

en/ visa-service/ -/ 231148

If you need a visa to enter Germany, please let us know as soon as possible so we can issue an invitation. The German Embassies or Consulates in your home country issue visas.

For the visa invitation, please provide the following information:

Name as it appears in your passport (first name, family name), Date of Birth (dd.mm.yyyy), Current address

Registration Fee

As mentioned on our website, as well as during the application process, a registration fee of 100 euros needs to be transferred. Upon arrival in Germany, the fee will be returned to you in cash. Please transfer the application fee as soon as possible, at the latest until July 8th, to this account:

Account Owner: LZK M-V fur Universitat Greifswald

Name of Bank: BBK Rostock

Address: Richard-Wagner-Straße 2, D-18055 Rostock

IBAN: DE26 1300 0000 XFTR CVXFD VX

BIC (SWIFT code): MARKDEF1XYXYY

Payment Reference:712115XYXYXYX – **Name Participant**

You will receive a confirmation as soon as the University has received the money. Please note that processing the fee can take up to ten working days.

Travel Information

Your scholarship covers a fixed rate which differs according to the country of departure. In your case, for India, the scholarship covers 1050 euros for the travel expenses. So for you, it means that you would book and arrange your travel, and once you are here, we will transfer the mentioned rate to your account. Your travel destination is **Greifswald**. *Since Greifswald does not have an airport, we recommend* **Berlin or Hamburg** *as the closest bigger airports. From these two cities, trains run regularly to Greifswald.*

Accommodation

The scholarship covers accommodation in full. The address of your accommodation in Greifswald is Maritimes Jugenddorf Wieck GmbH Greifswald Yachtweg 3 17493 Greifswald/Wieck.Check-in: Sunday, August 21ˢᵗ, between 2 PM and midnight in Greifswald. After four nights in Greifswald, your second accommodation will be located in Stralsund. Here you will stay for the rest of the programme. Checkout: Thursday, September 1ˢᵗ, in Stralsund Please plan your journey accordingly.

Daily Expenses

In general, your responsibility is to cover personal daily expenses and meals. However, some restaurant visits and catering are part of the programme, which the scholarship will cover.

Insurance

The scholarship does not include insurance coverage. Each participant is obligated to have health insurance that is valid in Germany (preferably Europe).In addition, we recommend accident- and liability insurance. The student is liable for all culpably caused damage, especially for damages in arranged accommodation. It is important to note that medical care in Germany can be expensive if you are not secured by insurance. In some countries' citizens must provide proof of insurance when applying for a visa. It is also possible that German customs will ask for proof of insurance when you cross the border. Please check with your insurance plan to see if it covers Germany. If not, every student is obligated to acquire some.

Congratulations again, and please do not hesitate to get in touch with us in case of questions or concerns.

Your SustainMV 2022 Team

* **

Carmen Opolski & Elisabeth Reich.

Programme Management SustainMV

International Office University of Greifswald & Rostock

Tel. + + 493834XXX1XXX

https:// sustainmv.de/

E-Mail: info@sustainmv.de

...

The next big thing in my head was not the end-of-semester exams but rather "The Process." I started dreaming while in Europe and enjoying as we usually watch Movies. There was so much running in my head. After two days, when I sat down and reread the email and understood well that I still needed to do many things. These whole things I called" The Process." Because it included many things right from the scholarship application fee of 100 euros which was to be given back to the candidate after arrival in Germany. Visa processing because I was an African who needed a visa to travel to Europe. Insurance, Flights, and personal amounts in case I see a good item and want to buy it. The mail also informed me whether I needed a visa to travel to Europe; I should send them a reply to get an offer letter which will help me in visa processing. I replied that very time, and I needed one, and I got it in four days well written and stamped, but it was in the German language, and I had to use google translate to get the meaning.

CHAPTER TWO

The Process

Many events happened in my life during the initial, transient, and final stages of the process of going to Europe; I lost friends and got chucked by my family. This stage really crushed me a lot, and it also opened me to the hearts of many people in my life. Some people pretend to be helping us while others pretend to be our friends. I got many back-off from people I thought would help me and cuddles from people I thought would not mind. The many things that happened stayed with me past to learn from and dreams to enjoy while other nightmares scare me and wake me up in the deep night to remind me that I have to sleep less and focus more on the present so that my future can be bright. I got to know how people see me; where many saw me as garbage, and a few saw me as gold. Those who hurt me wanted me to fail in this process, and those who cuddled me without backstab wanted me to flourish. I treasure more someone who never helps because they don't have or they cant than someone who never helps because they feel jealous. Life taught me many but I claim to remember few and those are the best moments and memories of good things that i passed through. I stayed with the box of past experiences as a dictionary, a reference to my present life, and guidance to the future that I don't know exists. Many people in this struggle came to my refuge and few stood to watch me crave, the director research and consultancy Dr.R.Papu, my aunt, my mother, the president Gitam International student's association (Raheem Qudus), my classmates (BTCM, 2020 – 2023) and the other people who gave me emotional support. In this chapter I will try to show their relevance and in the next chapter that follows it.

The Initial Stages

As an enthusiastic and happy young man, I called my aunt the same day I got the scholarship and forwarded the offer email to her. She read through it and was also very happy. By this time, she was in my native country "Uganda." I told her to share with my mother because she is not on "dot-com," as we say. They were all very happy. Then my aunt told me to research how much the whole process will cost me because once the money is high, then I will have to seek other means otherwise I will lose the opportunity. That very day I went to the German embassy website and searched the requirements and procedure for getting a Schengen visa. I got the information I needed and then started making my budget. This budget includes the following things Application processing fee by VFS-Global Visa application fees Transportation to the VFS-Global center for visa submission, biometrics, and interviews Insurance (liabilities and Health) Minimum account balance of 500e Flights Registration fees of 100 euros which were to be paid before the 10th of the same month. Having drafted the budget and shared it with my aunt, was up to 2000 euros; she was shocked and advised me to try the institution and see if they could help me in funding my trip. The challenge was the Host institution was to give back only "Transport" money, but the rest of the costs were on me, and they estimated a rough amount of 1050 euros, just almost half the amount I had in my draft. I was shocked at that time because I thought my aunt will say it was manageable. That whole night I didn't sleep, and my roommate Mr. Tumwekwase Solomon asked me what was troubling me, and I couldn't tell. I never wanted to stress him as he was almost done with his MSc.Applied Mathematics course and was in travel preparations back home. Later the next day I was not fit for attending lecturers, so I got thought that if this opportunity was shared with us by the International Foreign Students

Directorate, then if I go to their office and make them see what the opportunity was, maybe they can in one way or the other try to help me. I just went to them immediately because I had no option at that time. Having reached their office, I met the assistant director "Mr. I. Vimal," and I explained the situation to him and he advised me to send an email to the director requesting a Hand-loan to attend the summer school, and after completion of the event, I will repay. It was really a good idea, and I was almost relieved. But, before I went with the Idea, he told me to first wait. He went into the director's office and talked with him after some minutes, the director summoned me. I went inside his office shaking and in fears. He asked me to explain to him everything and what I needed at the moment. I explained to him and further told him that the opportunity was shared to us from his office and I got a chance to be selected thus I request his office's support in any way. He told me to write a mail as his counterpart told earlier and then he will discuss with the other directors. What I forgot to tell you my listeners was that I had gotten an opportunity to be recruited as a young intern in the office of research and consultancy in my University. This had happened a few weeks after my completion the World Youth Forum 2021 where I was selected as a "Start-up" delegate for my University and I went to Egypt for a period of 10 days. This trip also is in another book called The Egypt Boy where I narrate all the experiences and the amusements in Egypt that I saw and enjoyed. Leaving Egypt trip alone, I was at this place working as an Intern for around 4 months which me and my aunt termed as "Cubicle". I was not active as I used to be at station, stressed and muffled. The other challenge was I couldn't talk to the director where I was working as an Intern because the previous week, he had travelled to London for a meeting which was expected to be over in three weeks. I was out of options. Then luckily I had sent him a mail regarding my start-up project which I wanted to start working on.

He had replied to me directing me to meet Sir. Vikas in VDC building we talk about it further. I went to this building with hope that when I tell Sir Vikas, he will suggest me any other solutions atleast having two solutions would be better than one. Reaching VDC, I met him and we talk about the project, and had a very good interaction. As he finished giving me a project mentioning slot, I told him about he opportunity I got to go to Germany and explained to him what I wanted at the moment. He was very calm and welcoming, that he showed me that there was hope for me to get financial aid. He first told me that as VDC they have a way of mobilising if there is any of the students who has got any calling like mine be it intern-ship, conference etc.. He told me all the details, later after a long talk he suggested me to try writing a mail to Sir Dr.Raja Pappu stating all the details and how you need help. After telling him that sir wasn't in office for the next couple of weeks, he ensured me that he will give him a call and inform him about that mail such that he can look into it. Only that statement was what I wanted to hear. Having gotten the second source of help, I then went back to my room and drafted the two emails and sent them to the respective directors. The director of International affairs replied first the next day by informing me that he needs to know how much I had in present time so that he can try to make a claim of loan for me from the university finance office else he can not help me when I don't have anything. I never had any amount in my account because I had taken more than four months minus receiving money from my aunt as she was in a Trying situation of her life and also working on taking a vacation back to my country. So this showed that this chance was hard to get through. I then kept waiting for the director of research and consultancy to come back from London. The time from receiving the offer to the time of the start of the event in Germany was approximately two months. The director was to take one week on those two months, so I kept waiting for him. This whole week when I was waiting for him, I never had a normal life, always in in deep thoughts and stress, I called many of my friends in UAE, Canada and USA to help me with money and I promised them to return it, but they never gave me. One thing I noticed as a student in a foreign land, is that if your scholarship doesn't give you stipend, then suffering is ultimate. Many of my friends were telling me that even if they gave me the money how would I return it yet I don't even work or get stipend. These people were right. I had no other options but to wait for the director to come back. The Sunday of that week, as I had gone outside for some coffee with a friend at around 7 PM I was an abnormal message on which showed that my account was credited with almost $300 and I was shocked. I kept asking myself who could have sent it. I never used the money waiting for someone to call me claiming that they wrongly sent an amount to my account and I was ready to give it back. The day ended and I went back to my hostel and no one was calling. It was on my head all night and the next day, I went back to the cubicle as usual when I am not as they used to know me. One of the senior finance officer called me and asked whether I saw my stipend for being an intern with them for the past three months. I told him, I saw a $300 deposit on my account yesterday. He said yes, that is your stipend, and you will be receiving $100 every month from us as an intern for the time of intern-ship. I was very happy and joyous. My mind directly reminded me of the registration fees that I had to pay before 10th. I quickly rushed to the bank Union Bank of India of which I had my account in. I asked them that I wanted to send money abroad to an institution. They told me NRO-accounts can not send money abroad, unless I get PAN which basically meant Permanent Account Number and getting it was very hard as it required many documentations and it was to take around many months to be processed. I was so shocked and got stuck in the bank. I then asked the manager whether anyone with these credentials can send money for me of

which he said its possible but there might be some parameters and
he further said, the branch which does that type of remittance is
around 20Km from our branch. At that time I couldn't go to the
bank because I had to first look for a person who can can help me
do this transaction. I went back to the director of foreign student
affair seeking his help. He never helped me but rather, he told me
as they have many charges on their accounts, so he cant do the
transaction for me, yet I had the money in cash and it was a
matter of his making the transaction and me paying him what ever
amount has been deducted. Again it was a dead end. The next day,
Mr.Vimal texted me on whatsapp to check on me and see what i
was on at the moment. I told him I cant send the application fees
because I don't have PAN and he also referred me to the director
of which he had refuse. I told him what the director had said and
he then told me that, from our college, they had selected actually
two people for the same scholarship. I was curious to know who
that person was and also I was so eager to know what course he
was doing because he was not from my institute. I asked him
where its possible for me and the other candidate to communicate
and arrange all the journey process together. He actually agreed
and told me to wait for the other person so that he can help me
with sending the money because he was having the required
credentials. I agreed. I went to take my lectures for that day. One
of my friends called K.Tarunsaw me not in good moods and I
seemed disappointed, I told him what was happening in my life
the past week and told him about the bank issues. He told me his
mother works in the same bank but different branch, and he will
ask and see if he can help me. I had to wait for him the next day.

Sending the Application fees

I had a rough long day and I was disappointed though at the end I was having Hope from my friend. The next day as usual I woke up and performed my daily routine and then went the cubicle for my intern ship having opened my email, I saw a reply form Dr.R.Papu and he told me to meet him office as he was back from his official duties and he wanted me to explain to him well because he saw the mail and Sir Vikas had called him but he wanted more explanation. My heart was biting so fast and I begun to shiver, because he was already in office by the time I reported and I was fearing to enter his office.I printed out the offer letter and went with it as a sign of proof and to show that the scholarship was legit. I entered his office and as a simple and easy person, he told me to tell him what was the problem and what did I want him to do. I explained to him and showed him the offer letter, he checked it and searched the "Hosting University" to see whether its true and existing and the signatories on my offer letter to confirm whether they are the true people . He told me that sometimes people are scammed and they inject in their money which later causes them stress and end up losing many things even their lives. He further said, he will look into it further and if he confirms it to be legit, he will once again call me to see how his office an help me on it. Later that day my friend had gotten a solution as his mother told him that he can send for me the amount abroad. I was very happy as I had almost hit two birds at once. I asked him what we needed to do the transaction as I was running out of time. He said we will go to the bank the next day. That very night I asked Mr.Vimal when the other participant will be coming and he said that he had gotten a delay in travel and so he will be available the next day of which that day was one day to the 10th that was the due deadline for sending the application fees. I was worried but not for him because he was an Indian and making the payment would not take much time and process. The next day me and my friend we never attended lectures, we went to the bank that could send money abroad and started the process of sending money. The first person we met at the counter pissed me off. The guy took our papers and made us wait for one hour, later he came and said we had old papers so we needed to fill the new forms, we did that hurrying so that the remittance can meet the deadline time in Germany. After filling the forms, these people went into lunch break, we kept patient and after one more hour, we waited and the same person came and started speaking in the local language of which I dont understand it and he was talking with my friend. He then said we can not make the payment abroad because I was not a family member to my friend claiming that only Indian to Indian abroad transactions are possible and even if he is sending on my behalf, my name should not appear anywhere in the paper or in reference. That once this appears, the SBI(State Bank of India) will not allow the remittance. I fumed in the whole bank asking them why they wasted five hours from our time without clearing this before we even sat and filled new forms. I told them why they never told us everything in the start because we explained to them everything. My friend tried to calm me down but it was all in vain as I was like sulphuric acid. The manager came and they tried but nothing till one person who was sitting once talked to the two us to analyse the situation and see what was the possible solution. The man told us it was possible but his colleague had not fully understood what we wanted. He asked for the documents and took then to action. At that time, the SBI abroad remittance section was closed as said by the bank and the man told us he will put the money into process then the next day he will share with us the transaction details. we agreed and left the bank. When the other participant came that evening, he was expecting to use an online transaction method of which it never worked and he called me that he will have to go to the bank and send it. I agreed and told him to ask whether he can pay for me as well. The next day I was eager to get information from the bank to see whether my transaction was completed or not. We kept checking on the bank guy every intervals of two hours. He then finally told us that once the transaction is processes, we will see a deduct of the amount on the bank account so we had to chill. At around mid-day, I got a call from the other participant and he told me he has been informed that he can not pay for a non-Indian citizen. I got so stressed and shocked, I called my aunt back home and told he what was really happening and I was requesting her to help me pay the 100efrom my country because only Indian citizens are allowed to send money abroad yet the deadline was in hours form that time. My aunt was stressed of where to get the money and it was almost late in my country and banks were almost closing, so she decided to tell my mother who had some money but it was not summing upto the required amount, she then went to the grand parents and requested for their help. My grands gave her some top-up and it made the required amount. I asked her to take help of my uncle and they rush to the bank and try to see of it can make the transaction. She was lacking internet subscription on her phone and I begged her to borrow and subscribe because I needed real-time communication. She rushed to the bank only to read five minutes to the closure they told her, they can only send the amount and it stays in process then on Monday it will be completed because the next day was weekend. I got so worried because the people hosting us in Germany had said that once the deadline for payment ends those who would have paid will be considered. I told her to rush to western union, and check if they can allow transaction. She rushed and reaching there her phone battery went off and she had to first charge for a while. At that instant, my friend received a message that the amount had been deducted from his account and he received the receipt of payment. I can not explain the happiness I had and the relief but I was so thankful to God that it was only his powers that can do such a thing. After about 30minutes my mother called again and she was asking the details with the urge to send the money. I told her to leave it as there was someone whom I did not expect had paid for me. She was very happy and relieved because it was a stressful moment for all of us. Having got the first bit completed, I had to start brainstorming on funding and visa which were the main retardation factors in this journey. I then took my dinner and sat on my computer and started checking my emails. Dr.R.Papu had summoned me to his office the coming week to discuss more on the issue as he told me that it was legit and it would be useful for me as I had explained to him. I was so happy and got to my knees and prayed to God on the blessings he grants to keep adding and I also thanked Him that no miracle is big in his eyes. The whole weekend was so good for me and I was so joyous as a poet will, I was full of beans.

Getting Funding

The week after the weekend, I went to the office of Dr.R.Papu and he had gone through my case with some of his friends and confirmed that it was legit. He then told me that he was to help me with funding from his office. He asked for an estimate of the amount I needed and when it is needed as well as a detailed accountability for each amount as he is to sanction it from the finance. I was very happy as a king. Remember I had made my budget before, not leaving where I was sitting, I emailed him the budget which he attached to my previous mail and the offer letter. He further mailed them to his secretary for further processing. Then he told me I will be contacted by the secretary to finish all the process. I can not describe Dr.R.Papu because I had nearly known him for less than a year. He recruited me as an Intern, from no where without application but one thing he told me was that one of my professors who saw my love and desire for research and education had recommended me. My story with Dr.Papu will never be understood and I myself cant understand because its only God that puts us in any position He desires. I can never thank Dr.Papu enough but I rather thank God for all these favours in my life and for those who read all my previous books will bear me witness. That very day, the secretary called me and asked me to redraft an email that is well elaborated and clearly stating the amount I needed and the purpose plus attaching the budget I had made. I did that in about one hour or two. The email read:

Greetings sir,

I am K. Idrisa, student of Bsc.Biotechnology (IV sem) reg no. 122012301XXX, Uganda by nationality. I have secured a fully funded opportunity to represent Gitam University in Germany (this opportunity was shared by GCGC and International Office)in Sustainability projects and research, though its a reimbursement fully funded opportunity summing upto 1500e. This amount will aid me in covering for travel bookings(1000 euros), application fees (100 euros), visa application fees (around 90 euros) and insurance for 14days When the program is finished, the amount will be reimbursed to me and I will duly pay it back to your office. I here by request to know if there is anyway I can be helped by Gitam University as I will be representing the University and my start up project too in the Sustain MV. Summer program 2022 in Germany. Through this opportunity I will add to my entrepreneurship knowledge on the different scale up processes, exploring different ventures from different universities, learning new technologies and networking for my start-up because different universities have different start-up like Carbon footprint management, Chemistry from harnesses light, sustainable fuel from the sun and garbage. As for the University, I will be representing it enhancing it's external relations, recognition and advertising its A+ academic accreditation to the world. I will be grateful when my request is considered and any help will be highly appreciated.

Thank you

I sent it and she told me by tomorrow your request will be forwarded to the registrar and other respective authorities for approval. I was so happy and kept praying to God that my request gets approved. That very night, I called my aunt who was at my native place and I told her about the good news that happened in my life for the past seven days. The first thing she asked before I even told her was, why I took long minus communicating to her, she was worried about me. I explained to her what happened and how the director who gave me an intern position has accepted to support my travel. I know all you are waiting to hear how much money I was to be given. Now the budget I had was claiming 2000 euros but when the director talked with me, he analysed and said his office will help me with 1500 euros of which I had to get the 500 euros as approximately it was personal expenditure. I agreed even though it was not the amount I needed, but it was more than half. But one challenge was I had to give it back when the event was done because it was from the institution not his pocket. I accepted the offer and then decided that I wont have personal expenses that will be more than 200 euros. When I told all this to my aunt she was happy and called my mother instantly, told her the good news and they all were chanting prayers and testifying the power of God. The next days I was always checking on secretary to know what step the process is because I was an intern in their office, time reached when I was really too much in asking and she told to relax once the process is confirmed, she will let me know and share with me my sanction copy. I waited for about three days and before the end of the forth day, she came to my station and gave me the sanction letter and told me in about two or three weeks, the money will be in my bank and I can start the process. I was the happiest and I had to tell this to my aunt because she the lioness of my life. I always share with her much of my joy and difficulties and being that she is so prayerful and positive, she encourages me so much. I told her and she told my mother, the same situation of prayer chanting came back and they were all calling out for more blessings to fall upon us all. That very night I slept calmly and I was so peaceful. At this part the portion that was much huddle came to pass. I had to wait to see the amount in my bank after two weeks.

The Visa Process I

The next day, I contacted the other candidate whom we were selected for the same scholarship and I told him we need to start the visa process as soon as possible because when I checked on German-website, it showed that the visa processing time was about 15 to 20 days. This approximates to three weeks of which we had about one month and a half. When I told him, he was not that active and he was so lousy, so I started collecting the documents for visa process. The schengen Visa requires many documents those who have applied for it can acknowledge it. Around ten legal documents were required of which some took many days to be processed like the **NOC**(No Objection Certificate) which was to be issued by the registrar and it had to go through a chain of protocol before it could be processed and given out. This alone has a whole booklet of events which happened of which some were hurtful and others were memorable. I also had to get a 3months bank statement, a visa request letter written by me, an invitation letter from the host organisation of which I had gotten, the flight reservation, Insurance from a trusted source which covers Europe, Proof of residence and admission because I was a student, my stay visa copy because I was a foreigner and the visa processing fees of around 80e. This process was not easy and it was challenging.

Obtaining the NOC

At Gitam University everything has a given lengthy protocol in which it has to pass through, this protocol takes hours to days depending on the availability and sensitivity of the process. With my request for NOC, I went to the Director Foreign student's affairs of which Mr. Vimal had told me that the NOC is issued by their office. On reaching the office, I spoke with the director and he told me to send a request email to my HOD (Head of Department) then he will forward my request to the principal and then to the dean, the dean will then forward it to the registrar who will take his time looking through the need for NOC and the documents attached with the relevance of my trip to my course then once its satisfactory he will summon for the processing of the NOC and I can get it in about three working days. This process would take me time and thus what I did was to draft an email and send it to the authorities (Dean, cc to Principal and HOD) so that once the HOD fails to deliver my request, the two other people can help me. It was like passing through the whole protocol with a "portal". The email read as follows:

Greetings sir,

I am K. Idrisa, student of Biotechnology (Bsc, BTCM) reg no. 1220123010XX. I hereby request for a no Objection letter from your office to aid me process a Germany visa to represent our university in the Sustain MV summer school from 22nd August to 1st September 2022. This was an opportunity shared by international students office and GCGC in which I applied and got selected for the above program, on site under a reimbursement scholarship process.

Thank your sir.

The next day the Dean sent a reply mail to the principal giving him a go forward with the NOC process. So i had to just wait for some days. The next day, I asked my fellow participant (D.Sampath) and asked him what he was working on at the moment, he was actually not bother at all thinking he has a lot of time to process all the things he wanted for the journey.I told him, I was currently working on the NOC and if he gets time he should work on his as soon as possible because it takes time to get it. After the Dean's reply, the principal called me to his office and asked me the details of this travel and why it was important to my education and future career. having explain everything, the acknowledged and send it for processing in his office,and he told me to come back the next day. The next things was that I missed all my lectures for that day and from the time I started processing the visa documents I was never good at attending classes and neither was I in class even if I was present. I was always in search for the missing piece in my puzzle as the norm is most embassies once anything is missing, they reject visa, I never wanted this to happen. The next day I went to the principle's office and they had not even started on my NOC, they gave me some papers that I should take them to the HOD to write some recommendation and draft of the NOC, I hurried because our HOD was always busy and if he is in office, we must be very tactile with him. Reaching the HOD he said I should go to the assistant principal and talk to him, now that made be so angry as if they were playing me a fool. I went back to the principle's office and fumed, I told them why they fool me to the extent that they all don't know what to do so they want me to go on oozing like rubbish. One of the people called the office manager who came in to save the day. He calmed me down and told me the principals office doesn't issue out NOCs its only the registrar's office. He further told me that my NOC request was forwarded by the principal to the registrar, who ordered it to be made thus the next I will get it. He told me to leave my phone number once its ready, he will call me and I pick it. I did so and left the office. Reaching to class I remembered I had to draft the Visa request letter, I used that time to draft it and once I went back to my room I typed it and was ready to print it. It read as follow:

July 16, 2022.

EMBASSY OF THE FEDERAL REPUBLIC OF GERMANY

Hoechst House, Nariman Point,

Mumbai 400 021, India

Subject: K. IDRISA, Ugandan Passport No. A00245XZXX, Schengen Visa for taking part in the Year's Summer School Sustain MV of the universities of Greifswald, Rostock, Wismar,Neubrandenburg, Stralsund and Hochschule fur Musik.

Dear sir/Madam,

I hereby submit my application for the Schengen Visa upon my intention to travel to Germany from August 20 to September 3, 2022. The purpose of my travel is to attend the Year's Summer School Sustain MV of the universities of Greifswald, Rostock, and Wismar. This will help me learn more about sustainability, innovation, and research development as a young developing scientist from the Professors and scientists. Furthermore, I will get the opportunity to visit some of the best cities in Germany, interact with people from different countries, and experience German culture as well. I am an international student at Gitam University Visakhapatnam Campus, offering my Bachelor's of Science in Biotechnology, Chemistry, and Microbiology in my third year. My university has approved me for attending this summer school, and attached are the documents to support my visa application.

1. visa application is duly completed, dated, and signed with a passport photo attached.

2. Passport.

3. Travel Insurance.

4. Flight tickets reservations.

5. Invitation letter from Rostock university clearly stating my scholarship and its coverages.

6. No objection Certificate from my current university.

7. Indian Visa extension for my student visa.

8. 3 months bank statements I will be very grateful when my application is considered.

Thank you.

K. Idrisa

2XXX, santhi Zadan Hostel,

Gitam University, Rushikonda Visakhapatnam,

Andhra Pradesh, 530045, India.

After two days I never received any call from the administration, I went direct to the registrar's office and approached the PA, I told him I wanted my NOC, I was to get it two days back and I never received it. They started claiming that they were not given any orders to make one and they were trying to fool me. I just angrily told them I wanted to see the registrar. The PA was rejecting and I was angry, he started lying to me that he was in a meeting and I could come back after two hours, I as not listening to anything at that time. I was forcibly going into his office till when the PA stopped me and went it to inform the registrar whether he was free to receive any person, the registrar asked him who I was and he just said International student, then i was allowed in. I explained everything to the registrar who told me that he ordered his office to make for me NOC but maybe the person did not report for work but in about two or three hours I will receive it. I was calm and trusted the registrar with my heart. I went out and I worked on other documents checking for the time. After two hours I received a call from the registrar's office and I went to pick the NOC, it read as follows:

F.No: GDU/CXX/R/NOC-SustainMV/lLXX/12022 06-07-2022

NO OBJECTION CERTIFICATE

This is to certify that Mr K. IDRISA (Registration Number 122012XXl0XX) is a bonalide student of GITAM (Deemed to be University),studying 3 rd year B.Sc (Biotechnology,Microbiology and Chemistry) program during the Academic Year 2022 – 2023. The University does not have any objection to Mr K. IDRISA's participation in the SustainMV – 2022(On-site program) to be held at the University of Greifswald and Rostock, Germany from 22nd August 2022 to 1 st September 2022 The student, Mr K. IDRISA, will come back to India after completion of the On-site program held at Germany, so that he will pursue his B.Sc Program at GITAM.

Registrar (Dr. D.Gunasekaran)

GITAM UNIVERSITY VISAKHAPATNAM

The journey to visa processing was 25% over and then the hunt for the remaining documents was on.

The 1st *Visit at VFS-Global*

It took me another four to five days to collect the remaining documents like insurance, I did not know which provider to choose and the ones which were recommended were a little expensive but them I got Dr. Walter (Provisit Visum insurance),which was highly recommended for schengen travel. I had all the documents and then I applied on-line for visa filling in all the required information and after I was given the print out of the form. I had to print out all the documents and file them. Having done all that and collected all the documents required I contacted Sampathi to see what what stage he was on. sadly he had not started at all. I told him that we are running out of time if were are to go together. He was so lousy and reactant in the process, I told him to come at college and I show him the documents re is to have for visa processing. He claimed to be sick and he could not move, I was not satisfied till when I told him to come so that we work together. I waited for him in my hostel for long but he was not always good at time management, he came late and then I was having no problem but to show him what he needed to have. He was always being disturbed by I don't know who? but he claimed to always be busy of which I could not reject. So I told him to go make a file of all the documents because we need to schedule an appointment with VFS-Global for interview and biometrics. He agreed and went back to his home. That very night, I went to VFS-Global site and the earliest slots they had for schengen visa was in September 20th yet out program was in August -September. But they had an option of Walk in submission. So we thought we could do that and get our visa processed. I immediately texted Sampath the next day informing him what I got to know yesterday. But I then told him we needed to go to try a walk in submission without appointment. He was frightened so was I but me I have a strong heart, will and belief because I always have HOPE. I told him we needed not to waste time and thus we had to go the following day. Our college is located in visakhapatnam and state of Andhra Pradesh, thus our nearest VFS-Global center was Chennai and it was also recommended on their website that for our state we must use Chennai visa processing center. so we had to travel a distance of 795Km and the cheapest means of transport we had was Train but it was already booked and full so we had to use bus. Before I forget, where did I get the flight reservation?. Earlier when Sampath came to my hostel, he had made flight reservation which were cheap and i begged him to talk to his friend who helped him reserve the flights to also help me as well, he did it and the good thing about him was they had Dimes and connections, that's what I was so eager and in loving to travel with him. So we planned to leave the next day in the afternoon such that we reach in the morning and go direct to VFS-Global in Chennai. In the afternoon of that day I called the Germany embassy in Chennai and explained my problem to them which they told me to send it in a mail and they will get back to me. the mail read:

Greetings sir/madam,

I am K. Idrisa, student in Gitam University Visakhapatnam. I was recently selected for Summer exchange program at the University of Rostock, Greifswald from august22 to september1.

Having collected all the required documemts, the VFS global slots for visa appointment had the earliest slots in October21 which is far when the program is done. I hereby request a slot from your office in-between July and August so as to aid me get a visa and attend this program.

Thank you

In the evening I got a reply from the embassy which was so socking and almost took my Hope away but I never told Sampath because he could reject going and call it a dead end. The reply from the embassy was:

Dear Sir/Madam,

We know how important it is for you to schedule an appointment for your visa application as soon as possible and to receive the subsequent decision. We are aware that the Corona crisis has made your situation and the urgency of your visa application even worse. Families were separated, jobs were lost, planned study trips could not be started and private and professional plans were drastically mixed up. For many people, entry into Germany has therefore become even more important and urgent. However, even months after the outbreak of the pandemic, normality is still a long way off and travel restrictions, quarantine regulations and restrictions on our everyday lives are still or partially in force to contain the pandemic. This applies worldwide, but also especially with regard to the local infection situation for India. Corona influences naturally also the work of the German General Consulate in Mumbai. We are in a constant balancing act between protecting the health of applicants and our employees on the one hand and maintaining the range of services offered by the visa section on the other. As part of this balancing act, the Consulate provides the largest possible number of appointments in order to keep waiting times as short as possible. Nevertheless, longer waiting times for appointments cannot be avoided despite the best efforts of all consulate staff.

(Please be informed that all Schengen visa applications filed at VFS centers in Chennai, Pondicherry and Hyderabad will be processed by the Visa Section of the German Consulate General in Mumbai. The procedure at the concerned VFS centers will remain the same.)

For information regarding Schengen visas kindly find the updated information on the website https: //india.diplo.de/in-en/ vertretungen/gkmumbai/visaservices/2001006

Best Regards

Visa Section

Consulate General of the Federal Republic of Germany No. 9 Boat Club Road, RA Puram, Chennai 600 028 Tel: +91 44 2430 1600 Fax: +91 44 2434 9293 E-Mail: visa@chenn.diplo.de Web: www.india.diplo.de

We boarded the bus as I told you earlier that Sampath had Dimes, he paid for the cub to the but station and also booked the buses. This was my first time in a Sleeper bus. It was nice with A/c and beds were not smelly. So we just had to sleep for 15hrs till Chennai. the journey was long and intense. The good thing we had power and we could charge phones, laptops and even watch TV, but only Indian channels were available. I talked with my friends at college telling them where I had gone in-case the lecturers ask for me, I constantly talked with my aunt and my mother. Basically am good at giving updates.

We were to reach at 8 : 00AM but due to bus delays and the stops we made for refreshments and food, pieing and Number 2 they all made us reach at 10 : 00AM. We reached in Chennai and we had to take another transport mean to the VFS-Global office I thought we would use auto, bike or cub but Sampath made me take my first Tram in India as he told me he was an intern in the Tram-management and he also had a subscription card, so me I had to pay for the ticket. He showed me how the process should be and it was all smooth. We were on a hurry and after the tram we had to take an auto for the remaining journey. When we reached the Visa processing center, he was fearing to enter because many people were there waiting and stranded.I went to the entrance as you know in all countries in Africa and Asia, foreigners are not blasted even when you are to chase them away you must be polite. So I went and they officer was asking me the appointment letter, I just told me me and my friend we have a walk in submission from the embassy of Germany. He just let me pass and Sampath was still behind I called him. We went in without any appointment and reached the place where they checked our documents and I did the speaking in all. I told them everything needed and they told us to wait in the premium lounge for further processing. We went and waited, everyone was looking at Us like we were occupying their space. Having waited for several minutes the in-charge came in and told us that the appointments slots are not set by the Visa processing company "VFS-Global" but rather they come from the embassies. I told him we talked with the embassy and they know our situation. He told me that embassy can not give grant slot via phone call it should be a mail. I showed him the mail and clearly there was not statement that we were given special appointment but we were just trying our luck driven with HOPE. We tried to call the embassy many times and they did not pick. He finally got torn and we could not do anything at all. wasted transport, and the efforts we injected in for the processing all was causing us pain. We were all silent and we left the center as losers. we got the auto and went back to the bus station. Sampath decided to go back that day as he claimed to have many things to do and I stayed in Chennai for one more day. Because I knew there was still HOPE. Before sampath left, I had to pay him the money we he used to book for the bus and the room where I was to stay, but he also stayed for some three hours and we got some food, and refreshed and then jazzed a little and he told me how he had injected into this travel a lot with hope and desire for adventure. After some time he went and boarded back to University and I stayed. I slept for about two hours and them woke up and opened my laptop and I had some assignment I was to submit before the next day. I did it and my mind was really thinking a lot and I called my aunt. We talked and I told her about what happened that day, she advised me and told me not to lose HOPE and keep wishing for the best. This phone call was like therapy and boos to my brain and at that time I got a thought of contacting the organising team of Sustain MV. Little did i know that they had sent me a mail confirming that my 100ewas received and they were expecting to welcome me warmly. That mail echoed in my head and told me that I must go to Germany and I should Try all means and ways. When I sad on the computer, I never knew what to write in the mail, but after some time I wrote a mail that I don't know how I started it and how it ended but i remember seeing mail sent . the mail read:

Great,

Thanks for letting me know!

However as per Germany consulates in India, the only available appointment time for visa submitting are in October Thus I can't get visa on time I visited the embassy and all the visa processing centres, the only possibility they gave was the inviting university to send a mail to the embassy in Delhi for a special appointment allotment. Otherwise without that, I can't get visa on time and come for the program. Help me with the required help

Thank you

Having sent the mail, I slept because it was night and my heart calmed down the way i could not expect due to the stress We got in the morning. I woke up in the morning with a peaceful mind and heart. I took shower, and prayed to the Lord. I then looked for what to eat. Having done that I sat on my laptop and did my remaining work and submitted it. Then I booked the bus back to College.I never thought of the Visa issue any more and I was calm and peaceful till college. When I reached, I just started my routine for classes and helped my room-mate who was soon going back home. He also had some challenges which were almost hindering him from going back but luckily he finished them. Two days after I received a mail from the Sustain MV committee saying they will try to contact the embassy requesting for us a special appointment, the mail I received was reading:

Dear Idrisa,

Please let us know the contact information (email address) of the embassy so we can send an email concerning your appointment. Kind regards, Carmen

** ***

Programme Management SustainMV

International Office

University of Greifswald

Domstraße 8, 17489 Greifswald.

Having sent the information required, I resumed on helping my room-mate go back home and we took him at the airport the next day.The Sustain MV coordinator sent a mail to the embassy which was reading:

Ladies and Gentlemen

As part of a joint summer school of the universities in Mecklenburg-Western Pomerania on the subject of sustainability, two students from Gitam University in India were selected to take part in this program, which is a DAAD-funded project. Now Ms. Idrisa K. and Mr. Sai Sampath Dangeti informed me that unfortunately they would not be able to get an appointment regarding a visa before October. The summer school takes place at the end of August and it would be, so the students were told, an opportunity for me to contact you directly, which I am doing here. Both students were selected from a large number of applications for the scholarship and we would be very happy if you could still get an appointment for the visa. Please let me know if I can be of any assistance. The invitations, issued by my colleague from the University of Rostock, are also attached.

Thank you for your efforts and best regards from Greifswald!

Carmen Opolski

* **

Program Management SustainMV

International Office

University of Greifswald

Domstrasse 8, 17489 Greifswald.

I had to just keep waiting for the reply from the Embassy as I kept on praying and I also informed my family as well.

The Visa Process II

The next day I received a cc mail reply from the embassy of which the Sustain MV coordinator has sent to the embassy. The embassy was emphasising the fact that it is not possible for it to give us any appointment. I was really shocked and then the stress episodes came back.The reply from the embassy was as follows:

Dear madam/sir,

With regard to your query on Schengen visas, all Schengen visa applications filed at VFS centers in Chennai Pondicherry and Hyderabad will be processed by the Visa Section of the German Consulate General in Mumbai . The procedure at the concerned VFS centers will remain the same. So, kindly get in touch with VFS or the German Consulate in Mumbai at visa@mumb.diplo.de.

Regards,

Visa Section

I greatly thank the Sustain MV team as they never stopped trying. The next day Carmen (Sustain MV coordinator) sent a reply to the embassy informing them as they are the only ones to grant us visa appointment because she had sent VFS an email and they confirmed so. The mail was stating as follows:

Dear Sir or Madam,

Greetings from Germany!

I contacted the VFS center in Chennai on behalf of two students who need a visa appointment for a summer school in Germany which already takes place at the end of August. The visa center now replied that I need to get in touch with you:Below please find the email I sent

*to the VFS center on Wednesday explaining the situation. Please let
me know how I can support the process. The matter is quite urgent as
the summer school already takes place in a few weeks.*

Thanks and kind regards,

Carmen Opolski

* **

Programme Management SustainMV

International Office

University of Greifswald

Domstraße 8, 17489 Greifswald

All we had to do was to keep waiting. After some two days we
were not getting reply and I was really out of patience that I email
to the Sustain MV telling them that:

Greetings sir/madam

*Would you advise me to take the October visa appointment slot and
then share with you the necessary details such that you help request
the embassy to pre pond my appointment before end of July or
beginning of August. Because the time frame of 3 weeks visa
application is decreasing rapidly.*

Thank you.

I was given the above advise by the Director of International
Student's affairs, that when he was to travel to USA, his
appointment was not to happen as the slots were in a far date and
yet his programs were in the nearest dates,so he asked the hosting

institution to allow him take the far appointment time but for them they will email the embassy and it will inform VFS to allow him to take the appointment in time. This is what he used and it sounded like a good idea. Having sent the above mail, I got a reply from Carmen which was showing that she has really tried but maybe things are not on our side, her reply was as follows:

Dear Idrisa,

I contacted the embassy in Mumbai this morning. You are in cc. This is all I can do at this point. Let's cross our fingers that you will get an appointment quickly.

Kind regards,

Carmen

* **

Programme Management SustainMV

International Office

University of Greifswald

Domstraße 8, 17489 Greifswald

After around three days, without any reply from the embassy, I was now losing my will power and HOPE, I then contacted Carmen and told her how I was about to give up also and leave it as Sampath has done because he was not even bothered at all. He told me on the day we went for appointment and we never passed through that he is done and he is not going to entertain anymore stress. I rather asked me one thing was to keep the Flight reservation PNRs active. So I sent a mail reading:

The challenge is, VFS concealed the information that it is the one entitled to schedule appointments and rather informed that the embassy was the one doing so. Yet the recent reply from the embassy in Mumbai shows that VFS is the one mandated to schedule appointments.

This all creates doubts and questions, and I think we have no other options, and the tickets we had bought, should be cancelled, insurance as well. Which is a big loss from us as students because the university never injected in anything for us. How about the 100 euros we paid for registration which was to be handled back in cash ? Thank you, for everything event though, we didn't get appointments but you(the team) has tried a lot.

At the same time I had sent a mail to Dr.R.Papu informing him of what was taking place in the process of Travelling to Germany.This time this mail will be left out because it really made me look like a hopeless person. I was crying childishly and even Dr.R.Papu's reply was so positive that he was like knowing what will happen yet he was noticing me crying and losing hope in my mails. Carmen replied to my mail as follows:

Dear Idrisa,

I did what I can do ... did you hear anything from the embassy concerning an appointment? In case that due to the visa issue you will not be able to attend we will of course reimburse the 100eand transfer it to your account. But maybe let's still wait a little bit. Maybe you get an appointment on a short notice. I cross my fingers! Maybe try calling them again?

Best wishes, Carmen

** **

Programme Management SustainMV

International Office

University of Greifswald

Domstraße 8, 17489 Greifswald

When I saw this mail I was really hopeless and I went to the Director Foreign student's affairs and asked him for another advise, he told me to try applying for visa in France or Italy because those are schengen areas I can travel to Germany with their visa as well. He was right about that because he told me his family friend once faced the same challenge and they did the same thing and they went. But to me as a young traveller, I looked at the documents required for France and Italian visa, they were all not easy to get and more so they invitation letter I had was for Germany. So I relaxed and removed the Germany journey in my head for the moment. One person once ever told me that "If God wants you to get something great in your life, He first prepares you for it. He does so by bringing challenges into your life to see perseverance and trust-ship you have in Him. Once you display enough of it, He will open paths through which paths can not be made by anyone except the Lord most high" I remembered that and my head told me that "Idrisa, God is preparing you for something Big and the heavier the tests He gives you, the Heavier your Present is form Him." The Friday of that very week, I was in the Cubicle doing my own intern work as usual I saw an Unusual mail that read as follows:

Dear Opolski, Carmen In the case described, the German Consulate Mumbai will grant a special date/appointment for

submitting the application to our service provider VFS. To further process your request, we need the following data of the applicant/ s:

1. Surname:

2. Givenname:

3. Passport number:

4. Date of birth:

5. Place of residence in India:

6. E-mail:

7. Telephone number:

8. Please state at which VFS application center in India the applicants wants to submit his/her application: 9. Intended date of travel:

Please note that we can only process your request if the data above is completed. Please use this email for your answer. Upon receipt of your answer, the applicant will receive shortly an appointment confirmation from VFS via e-mail which will enable him to submit the visa application as the chosen VFS branch within the time-frame mentioned in that e-mail.

sincerely yours,

RK-S3 / Visa Section

Consulate General of the Federal Republic of Germany Hoechst House,

Nariman Point,

Mumbai 400 021, India

Phone: +91 22 2283 0XXX / +91 22 2283 98XXX.

I was very happy and almost felt like crying because indeed God was preparing me till the edge when I almost lost Hope.I immediately told Sampath to check the mail and Send his details to Carmen who will further forward them to the embassy such that we can get appointments. I sent my details and was now waiting. That very night I made a call to my aunt and I informed her about what happened and she was so happy and she called my mother immediately and told her to add more payers because the process is being managed by God Himself.I told her how i almost lost HOPE and I was having no peace at all. I could not do anything productive and even concentrate because I had expected the process to be smooth and yet it was not. She tried to calm me down and encouraged me to keep praying and never stop no matter what and she also told me to never lose **HOPE** because it never dies. That very night was special and I slept peacefully.

Having gotten the special visa appointment from the Mumbai consulate,our details were sent but there was something that happened on my details which till now I never understood. I told Sampath what to do but because he is lousy and doesn't listen to comprehend messages, he did the opposite of what I told him and then he replied to the embassy mail with his details yet it was addressed to Carmen not Us because we were just in cc to follow the progress of the process.We had to re-check our documents and re-draft our Visa cover letter. That step hindered me somewhere I will explain it in a new chapter. Above all we had this appointment and submitted out visa application and we had to wait for almost twenty days but we had only 19 days to go.

VFS approval for the appointment.

Having sent the details, Sampath was granted appointment that very day, he never told me. I waited for the weekend to end and then check to see if I would be given an appointment the following week. The Monday of the starting week, I was in my cubicle when I checked my email and I had not gotten any appointment approval. I called Sampath to ask him whether he got anything. He then sent me a screen shot of the reply email he had gotten the previous week on Friday confirming his appointment. I was so furious and asked him why he never told me about it but he had no answers. I quickly emailed to Carmen, that she sent two person's details but why one was granted appointment and the other was not. She never replied and I copied the phone number of the service desk from the screen shot he had sent, I called VFS-Global chennai, I asked then why they granted appointment to only one person yet two person's details were sent from the embassy. The lady on phone told that she had raised a ticket for my query and forwarded it to the manager, hence I had to keep wait for about eight hours to twenty four hours. I waited and went to class, took my lectures for the day. When I asked Sampath when he was going for the second time in VFS-chennai, he had planned and booked the train for the next day evening such that he reaches morning the following day. I was so stressed and tormented asking myself many questions till when I reached to a degree of saying maybe it was maybe because I am not Indian, but all were because of stress and the lack of coordination between me and Sampath. I even asked Dr.R.Papu what he though about it as he has travelled a lot more that I so he could guide me well, he just said one thing, "Visa issues have no bias and favouritism so be strong they will call you when you time is right."So what really happened was, Sampath sent a reply mail to the embassy mail which was seen the same day containing his details alone and the embassy forwarded it to VFS for further processing yet me I had sent to Carmen in Germany who took more than eight hours to send the details of me and Sampath. It was all Sampath's problem because he never listened to me and did what he wanted and more over if I had not wanted him to get updated with the info I would also have concealed the information about the special visa appointment. Leaving that a side. I asked him a favour which he accepted to do for me. I begged him to ask VFS when he reaches the appointment center why I never received appointment mail. The next day Sampath went to the center and I also called the center before he asked them, they told me my issue was still in process. When Sampath communicated to me, he said they had just not read the full email and thus I will have to go for appointment too, and he told me they had told him that I can come even without email for confirmation. I rejected and asked him to tell them to send me an email first. Then after some time I got the email which read :

Dear Idrisa,

Greetings from VFS Global!

We would like to inform you that you have been issued with a special appointment by the German Consulate General Mumbai for submission of your Germany Schengen visa at the Chennai Visa Application Centre. You can walk-in for submission of your visa application with a copy of this email to the Chennai Visa Application Centre between 08 : 30AM and 10 : 00AM from Monday 01ˢᵗ August 2022 to Friday 05ᵗʰ August 2022. Please note, the timelines for your submission have been set by the German Consulate Mumbai, therefore your walk-in appointment is valid only between Monday 01ˢᵗ August 2022 to Friday 05ᵗʰ August 2022 and we will not be in a position to change the dates.

Once I received the above mail, my heart was calm and I had to prepare for the second visit at VFS chennai. Sampath called me and he told me he had finished the process and all his documents were taken, biometrics and interviews. I was happy for him because he had lost HOPE. He was also happy but never wanted to show it, I also booked for the evening bus to chennai such that I reach in the morning.A few minutes, I called my aunt who at this time was back in Dubai for work, I told her,"mom, our prayers passed through as always, God is always with the patient and I have at last gotten the VFS appointment approval and I am soon heading there by today's last bus" She was so exited and told me to keep trust in God and always keep hopping for the best. We then talked about other things and even asked her about her sickness of stress, she was going through. So many huddles she has gone through and she is one of the Super-women I know. It is a 14hr to 16hr journey in bus. In my university hostel students have very limited room for movement minus administration knowing and the process takes a long time to get approval. I had only three hours left to departure of my bus. I sent a mail to all the respective departments and never waited for approval. As i was heading to the main gate to get out, I met the warden and she was asking me where I was heading and once I told her that at that moment I was heading to class but in around an hour I will head for chennai for visa appointment she was furious that I never followed protocol and I was also furious that she never confirmed my mail so we were all in fury mode. I just ceased the conversation and told her that I will pass via her office before I depart such that we sort out everything. Guess what I just head to the bus station after the lessons, my friend had a bike and was willing to drop me to the bus station, I couldn't miss the chance. I went and checked in then settled waiting for the bus to move.

Having gotten into the bus, I was just on prayers and my knees asking God to make it easy for me. I rechecked to see whether I had all the documents, I even had placed them in my file which was having a zip such that I can't lose any document once something happens unless I lose the whole file. I then took a nap as usual Sleeper buses. we drove for about four hours and they stopped the bus so that we get some food and piss even number two for those in need of it. In all the trips to chennai I only ate one type of dish Chicken Fried Rice because it was averagely spicy and I could handle it. Water was the most important thing and self entertainment. The bus reached at around 10AM yet the time taken to travel to the VFS offices was around one hour. I got out and stood at the road waiting for auto to come, they all were charging me highly because they saw I was not Indian. It suddenly started raining and I was left with no choice but to get into their trap. I got one guy who seemed to be good and charged me around 500rps. He wanted to show me that the amount he charged was very little so he took the heavy traffic road, yet I was racing time. He also used to drive while not caring and on phone calls, talking a lot and asking me many questions about my origin and reasons why I was in India as if he was the one to interview me. I felt so bad and I was really offended, then I decided to be silent. He continued to talk. after reaching VFS center I paid him the exact amount he asked before and he had refused it saying the journey was too long. I did not say anything but just kept quiet and out his money on this dash-board. I found many people stranded and others waiting for their appointment time as always. Many had come late and were not allowed in and others had not enough documents. I showed my appointment letter and I was allowed in, I expected to be treated like VIP because I was having a Special appointment from the embassy but nothing like that. I was sent into a long queue of people. The good thing was my name was on the list of special visa appointment, so I asked the lady passing by and she told me to just pass through the line and see the lady at the entrance. I did so and I was given a token number 34. I was then told that since I had not subscribed for premium, I must wait in the chair queue as others. I was directed to the queue of Germany visa seekers and I waited patiently. After one hour, Hunger started to play and I was feeling headaches, nausea and loss of vision because I had taken around 10 hours minus food. I waited till when my number was called and I was sent in for interview and processing. I thought the interview will be so difficult but it was a walk in a pack. I answered a few questions while they were passing through my documents and arranging them in order. After a few minutes I was asked to pay the visa fees, this was around 1000rps which included the VFS processing fees and courier. I was then told to sit and wait for biometrics. They always take the forms and data collected to be fed into the computer which is them sent to the embassy together with the hard data in a file. After around four hours of sitting, checked up to see whether my turn was next. The man told me it was still in processing, I was really hungry and not well. I tried to sleep but nothing. Suddenly the biometric scanner broke down and they called in the technician to repair and configure it back for functioning. We all go intimidated and people started saying where they came from and others had other local flights to take as they can't miss them. I was silent and after around one hours, the scanner was fixed and we resumed with biometrics. I was a little far, so I got a place next to the counter and hear well when my name is called. They called around two people and surprisingly my name was called third, my biometrics were taken and I was happy, I was then told that I will be getting updates on my phone about the visa processing at each stage. They requested for my delivery information, I gave it. I then walked out happy and smiling because I left people I met there then I remembered that I asked God to make the process easy for me and "Yes" He did. I walked out, and took an auto to the nearest bus station and the cheapest bus was for the late evening around two hours from that time. I booked it and I found somewhere to get some food and refreshments plus freshening up. I took a shower and ate some food, I tried to sleep but I have a habit of not sleeping when the sun is seeing me. So I never slept however much I was tired. I decided to make small tour around Chennai and compare it with my place (Visakhapatnam).

Chennai Tour

Chennai is a very big place and the place I was just a few meters from the bus station was having an over bridge which was built as a tram line for the city tram. It was so high and heavy and beneath it people were vending their crop items like fruits, food crops, and many others. The place was so hot at degrees of about 39oC and I had to carry my water bottle everywhere or else I would get dehydrated. I walked slowly observing the different places like Buildings, and parks. The only challenge I got was the smell of the city was awful that it made me develop nausea and I had not to take off my mask. I walked slowly observing the city life of people, some people were resting lying along the shades just a few meters away from the busy main road, others were beneath the shades created by heavy load trucks and a few of them were standing along side the road observing and counting cars. Many people were wearing in a naive way mostly the males (small cloth rapped along their belly region which lowered down a little to their knees but not covering them all) in which they could do their businesses in as a workwear. Many of the people were sole-traders and often laid their items in shade places like Fuel stations, Bus stops and others where often people came to take shade and would buy from them. Furthermore, cows were allowed to move freely in the city and highly respected. I almost got hit by a car because I was heading in the opposite direction of the cow and never did it even fear to move away but rather I was the one to move away. The parts of the city that I reached to were not so bad and showed to be developed but the challenge was the high levels of pollution that even the breathing air was not well filtered. Above all, visakhapatnam is better when it comes to sanitation, low levels of pollution and average temperatures. I enjoy my city because it is also silent but Chennai was really noisy and even the place I had taken a room the first time we visited had ceiling and when I closed the windows I could not sleep due to the loud noise that came out. To those who enjoy foods and other edibles, Chennai is a good place and they are cheap. I saw many fruits I had taken long minus seeing like Jack-fruits, Guava and Pea but I could not eat them because of hygienic reasons as the places where they were being sold fresh, many flies were the first guests to them even though they could pack them in polythene bags but it could not make me get the urge any more. After about one hour of walk I was back to the bus station and only ten minutes to departure, so I entered and took my bed, I put my phone on charge and slept because it was almost night as in India it gets dark very early. My eyes were still hovering in the windows to see how Chennai city looks at night but it was really nice as the many high rise buildings gave in a beautiful view with their lights on and the lights which were on all the side lit the city roads.

What could possibly go wrong

Having reached, Visakhapatnam in the morning at around 10AM, I had to get transport to the University. I ordered for fast bike and in about 15minutes I was at the University. I just sign in and reached my room, took a shower and I had to go to the cubicle because I had taken many days minus reporting. The supervisor asked where I was for the past two days and I had to explain my whereabouts. Having sat and opened my email, I go an update from the VFS visa company and the mail stated:

Dear IDRISA K.,

Dear Sir/Madam,

Your Visa Application Ref no GECN/030822/XXYY/01 has been received at the Chennai AC/OC.

I was happy, and I knew things were moving as the lord planned them. I then asked Sampath whether he was recieving update messages and he said he was. Later that night I talked to my aunt and narrated to her all what happened and she was calling me The special Visa appointee and we joked about that and I told her what I expected at the VFS center and what I got there, the huddles I passed through and how Chennai was. This aunt of mine, she is my mother, my sister, my friend and my bestie as well. I always talk with her and I picture many things and she keeps motivating me and always says Life is as you make it, so don't stop imagining and picturing, one day you will shade a good and clear picture that will post a high value in your life. Before I slept that night, I received a new mail from VFS reading:

Dear IDRISA K.,

Dear Sir/Madam,

**Your Visa application Ref no. GECN/030822/XXXY/01 has
been Forwarded to Mumbai on XX/08/2022**

I slept calmy and peaceful knowing that my visa will be processed
with in time and I will have the time to move with no delays. I was
just waiting for updates every time and nothing more to do but
rather to focus on the upcoming semester mid exams and my
lectures.

After some two days, we both were receiving similar mails, and
the next mail was telling us as our application was in Mumbai at
VFS center and we kept on waiting till when they sent us that our
application was received at Mumbai Germany consulate. However,
I received this mail before Sampath received his, and I told him
about it so he was asking me why and since I wasn't working in
VFS or embassy I could not answer him. Sampath had lend me his
plug for charging, so he wanted to pick and I met him at the
entrance of our mess-hall. We discussed about the visa issue and I
told him to be patient the visa will come in time and we will have
to rebook the tickets as the ones we had reserved are already
cancelled. The very night I talked with my aunt and my mother, I
told them to keep praying for me so that the visa comes in time
and I plan the flights once the visa is issued. Actually VFS was just
an intermediate in visa process but there was no guarantee that
once VFS processes you, Visa is granted, it was the embassy's
sovereign authority to grant or reject visa. The next day I went to
the cubicle in the morning, doing my stuff and feeling really not
comfortable, as I was about to get some coffee, my phone rang in a
very different way I never heard it ring, an unknown number
called me, I have one thing in my life that I pick up calls no matter
what, either I tell the caller I am busy to call later or I treat their
calls priority because I normally don't get calls from anyone

before prior information. The call went as follows:

Unknown caller: Hello! am I talking to K. Idrisa?

Me:Yes sir?

Unknown caller: I am having you schengen visa application on my table now, can you tell me why you want to go to Germany?

Me: Sir, I secured a DAAD scholarship to attend a summer school training for about ten days in Germany organised by the University of Rostock, Greifswald and HOST.

Consular: Okay! I can see. Now your documents show that you need to go by 22nd of this month, so you have less time.

Me: Yes sir.

Consular: Okay then, thank you for your time, I have forwarded your application for further processing and expect to get updates from VFS in about three working days. Have a good time.

Immediately the call ended I called Sampath and he never picked, hanged up and sent me a message that he will call me back.I waited for his call till 12noon when he called. I asked him whether he had received any call from the Mumbai consulate, he said he had not. I told him to always be ready because he might get an abrupt call from the consular as a final interview. I told him that they had called me in the morning and asked me the purpose of my visit to Germany. I then took my classes of the day and in the evening of that day, I called my aunt and we talked, I told her about the abrupt interview from the consular and how frightened I was when I knew he was the consular. We made many jokes of how I was and she asked me whether I pissed in my undies, and I told her that I was also in my cubicle in my chair rotating as a boss, but once the call came and I realised it was the consular, everything froze and the space shrunk and I was intimidated by his voice even you know the Germany accent. That day ended and I was waiting for the next updates. Sampath never got any call, and he asked me what I though could be the reason , I couldn't tell but what I told him maybe foreigners visa processing is different from citizens. The next day, I got update that my Processed Visa was dispatched from the embassy to Mumbai VFS site. I had to wait for quite a long time. The departure time of 22nd was almost near. Another thing was, all on-site participants were also entitled to attend the online event. So I had to do so as I wait for the my passport containing visa to reach. Sampath never got updates till, I got updates that my processed visa was flown to my city using Blue-dart and I was given the tracking number to observe its movement. I got all this information when I called VFS again asking them about the time of delivery of my passport containing visa. I also asked about Sampath's case but they claimed that I had no rights so it was the own who was to ask about it, of which they were right. At that moment I called Sampath who never picked and I was so furious because he sent me a text message that he is busy, he will call me later. I really felt bad because it was urgent and he never bothered to call in one or two hours but rather he called at around 10PM in the night. I had no words to describe him and neither did I have anything to talk to him but rather I decided to listen to him talking, then once he was done, and due to the anger I had, I was to go bad on him and when I am angry I don't talk at topic that made me angry. So I decided to just give him some advise because I realised it later that he was just a young boy who was resting in the body of a man. He claimed to be sorry but we could do anything, till when I told him to contact VFS the next day and check on the updates of his visa.

After few days, the online program had ended and within one week we had to go for the on-site program. My visa was on its way and I could check everyday the movement and expected date. The last tension came into play when I checked the available flights and the cheapest flights were in around 1lakrupees which was so huge and it was true because I was booking flights today and after one day I had to travel. Checking my account and the money which was sanctioned by the office of Dr.R.Papu was just half that needed for me to book flight. I was stuck, ran out of options and I told my aunt, she was also broke and had nothing to do at all. She just said that I pray to God so that He can make a way through the mountain I was facing. I prayed and could not sleep. I called my friend Raheem Qudus the president of our International Students' association in our University. I told him what I was facing and explained to him what really I wanted. He was not having money at all and we had two options, of which one was good because it had helped one time when I was stranded in my way to Egypt. This was To ask a PhD scholar whom we knew had some money always with him and since the trip was to give back the money after the summer school, we thought he would see it easy. Neither me nor Qudus wanted to talk to him, but since it was me in need I had to talk t him, Since he was a respectable man, I could not just bump into him, so I had to schedule an appointment with him hence I sent him a message after getting his number from his close friend. He agreed to meet me and I was waiting for his call as he told me he will send me a message once he was free.He never sent me a message and I was having only two days to going, I told Qudus about what happened and he was also shocked, but we had another plan, which was to call all the African brothers and we explain to them the situation so that we can collect any small amount we have. I agreed with the plan and he also told me about someone from Ethiopia who was also a PhD person and he was seen to have been helping people with some money. This was the guy I was ignoring all the time, and never wanted to be close to him because every time he wanted political discussions and advocating for rights stuff like that and yet I don't like such discussions. Now I had to face him and listen to his crap but then ask him what I wanted because I needed help. I went to his room that very night, he was so surprised to see me and very happy in a bad way. He gave me a sit and I started telling him why I was in his room that late. Having told him my problem, he reminded me of the way I ran away from him every time and he once told me to meet me and I refused. I expected all that he said and not in bad faith, I never wanted his company and just because I had a problem and yarning for help, he was the last person I had to go to. Having talked like for one hour, he told me he has no money as the amount I wanted was huge, and even if he could, he would not help me because I treated him badly. He then gave me advise but all was passing over my head and I was praying he finishes. Finally I went off his room and met Qudus again, I told him what had happened and he was surprised . The last option was to call for ever African man in the hostel.My visa was to arrive the next day around 11AM and I was waiting eagerly to see and touch, smell and kiss the First European Visa in my passport. Before I slept, I drafted a message which I sent to my class group seeking for their help as well. the message read as follows:

Greetings to you.

Rarely do I come to you my family for anything but this time I need your support how ever small it might be. I am having my trip to Germany on 20th but unlucky my flight ticket has some balance of 40krps I had all the required amount for the trip, but due to unavoidable circumstances which transpired in visa process I used more money that necessary. I hereby calling upon all of you, to help me by borrowing me any amount you can afford, which is going to be returned once I am back from the trip (Instantly.Because the host University (Germany) will hand back all the amount I have used in cash. Please help me I need you now.

The Rush days.

The morning of the following day, I checked my phone and around five people from my class had deposited for me some amount summing upto 6krps, it was a good start. Qudus had scheduled a meeting with all the African males in hostel at around 11AM and we were waiting for the time, when I finished to get my breakfast in mess, I was called by the courier from Blue-dart, that my passport was at the pick-up point. I rushed to go and pick it. I got it and opened it at the instant to see the whether Visa was granted or not and also to put the first eye on European visa. It was really looking different, because I was comparing it with the Indian Visa and Egyptian Visa I had in my passport but it was different. It was having the normal features of all visa (Photo and texts) but above all that, it had this embedded seal that lit silver every time light passed over it, the, it was duo-circular with DE and EU on opposite sides. I was the happiest at the moment and had I not been in a crowd of people at the moment I was going to shout out loud and run wildly. I sent my aunt a text that I had finally gotten the visa and the passport was in my hands, the immediate thing she told me was to send her the picture of the visa. I sent it and she was not believing that finally the time had come for me to again go for another international holiday.I went back to hostel reaching a few minutes before the start of the meeting. When the meeting started, Qudus addressed us and gave a brief reason for the meeting of which he called me to speak and tell the people what happened and why I needed their help. In my words I gave a brief introduction of the program I was going to, the way I got the program and what the scholarship was to cover on my program and how I needed to be helped at the moment. I emphasised the fact that once I will be back from Germany, I will pay everyone who borrows me their money at the present time. among the late comers was one of the other Ethiopian guy who I told you about earlier, he asked a very personal question that how would the program benefit him as a person once he helps me. I really never had an answer but I knew it was the grudge he had about me. I forged an answer not to look stupid but I was not ready for such personal questions in situations of need. Qudus then later asked everyone to pledge or lend me any amount they could afford with him starting the a specific amount and others followed while many of them told him to pass at their rooms in the evening, the truth was they never gave him anything, they could not say it that they were not willing to help neither were they not financially well. We collected amounts from 100rps to any amount, the total sum of amount collected from the people I stay with in hostel was around 6krps with a friend called Bertin, who contributed the most and I thank them all very much for the love and togetherness they showed to me when I was in need. After that incident, I sent a mail to Carmen in Germany telling her that I had gotten my visa and the flights were quite expensive as I was booking on the last minute, I was requesting her to ateast increase the travel fees, the next day before the journey begun, I received her reply and it was reading as follows:

Dear Idrisa,

Good to hear that you received your visa. Concerning the travel expenses: It was communicated from the beginning that we reimburse a certain amount depending on the country of departure once you have arrived here in Germany. There is nothing we can do about it at this point. Thanks for understanding and please let us know if you will arrive in Greifswald on Sunday.

Thanks and kind regards,

Carmen

* **

Programme Management SustainMV

International Office

University of Greifswald

Domstraße 8, 17489 Greifswald

In my class was a friend, Sri Vidya who was to touched by my call for help and talked with her parent who promised to help me with the remaining sum of money. At that time I was remaining with around 25krps, she called me and asked me how much money was remaining of which I told her and she promised to bring it the following day in cash. The night I was always looking at flight tickets changing every hour till when I could get the cheapest flight possible. Most flights of Lufthansa, Turkish Airlines, Brussels and many others were way high in laks of rupees. I kept on checking every hour till when I saw a flight which was average at around 80krps, but unfortunately I was lacking around 10Krps, so I had to wait for Vidya the next day and book the flight. I decided to prepare other things like COVID-certificate, PCR (just in case) and luggage. At around 1PM Vidya came to my hostel and handed me the money, I was so happy and I rushed to finishing the booking. The cheapest flight at that time was Polish air, and it was taking me to Poland (Warsaw) first then to Berlin. I booked it and got confirmation for booking in about five minutes. I was very scared because I used a secondary messenger to book (Make my trip) of which once the amount is deducted from the account and booking is not confirmed, refund was in 14days so I was so worried and stressed when I never got instant confirmation. Once I got it, I had to also book the local flights to Mumabi airport, I had even forgotten about it due to much stress. At this time Sampath was still waiting for his visa and we communicated, I told him to keep waiting and always remind VFS to see. After that I begged him to book for me the flight to Mumbai of which he agreed and lend me 7krps for the flight and I booked it. The journey was to start the next day because my local flight was the next day at around 6PM. That night I talked with my aunt I updated her on what was the situation, she was just happy and prayerful. We continued with our talk till when I was feeling asleep.

CHAPTER THREE

The Journey to Europe

The next day, I had to make official permissions to depart the University so I went to the warden's office and I told her that I was leaving for Germany. She was so surprised and asked me quite many questions of which I was not in moods to answer but later I answered a few of them. She then told me to ask my parents to send an email that they allowed me to travel to Germany, I should also share my travel tickets to her and the directorate of student life and then she will grant me permission to go. Immediately I contacted my aunt about sending the email of which she did in just a few hours. I also shared my travel tickets and the warden gave me permission to leave the hostel. After some few hours, I had to leave the hostel, I called Quddus to see if he would drop me at the airport but he was busy so I decided to go on my own. I had packed my things already, I grabbed them and went to the reception and I signed out. I rolled my suit case towards the main gate on reaching I showed the permission slip and I was allowed to go out. Having reached out, I knew that there was no going back. I stood outside like for few minutes then ordered for a fast bike. It took around five minutes to reach my location. I was waiting, wearing my hood-jacket and black stretchy trousers with my black watch on and my navy blue tight fit shirt. Having sat on the bike, the rider was so talkative and I could not enjoy the ride, he was asking me silly and annoying questions right from where I was coming from (basically asking for country of origin to why I was using a bike while going to the airport yet I am a foreigner). All these questions I could not answer them but rather I was quiet. I answered just few and left him to speak till the ride ended and he kept on calling his friends telling them he was taking a foreigner at the airport and they could not believe. The ride took arounf 40min due to the heavy traffic and finally I was at the airport.

I reached the airport 3hrs before my flight. The flight to Mumbai (BOM) was not scary and I was not frightened to board it because it was a local flight. I approached to the security check, showed my student ID and the office told me to show my passport. I asked him why and he claimed that I was a foreigner and only nationals are allowed to share their national identification document and student IDs.I pulled out my passport and showed together with my flight ticket, I was allowed in. I went for check it of which I had done online check in, so I was just taking my luggage for screening and tagging. It was done and I went to the respective gate for boarding. I waited for about two hours and during this waiting I received a call from my aunt as always she calls me at each stage when I am in travels.We talked and I explained her my travel map and she was happy and she kept saying I am praying for you my son. She also said one thing that she is fearing the flight from Mumbai to Warsaw but mostly the emigration part. This was true because during the Egypt trip, I n ever had a visa for travel but I had the remaining documents and I was rejected from boarding so it was still torturing all of us. This time I had visa and all other documents but something happen when we don't know and we are not in control of them. So we boarded the flight and It flew us for 1.5hrs to Hyderabad where we had a lay over of 2hrs before the final flight to Mumbai. At Hyderabad I looked for something to eat as I was very hungry and the only thing I could see was "Sweets", I just bought two to increase my sugar levels as I was tarting to lose focus and control. After a few hours, we boarded for Mumbai and it took around 1.5hrs to reach Mumbai. The good thing was I was dropped at Terminal 2 where I was to board for the international flight. So I was not to incur more charges to get transport to another terminal. I went out of domestic section and moved to international flights' section. I reached around 2hrs early and I had to do the check in faster but the initial process to check in was taking about 30min which was including security. I went into a long queue of people and we started moving like bread on an assembly belt.

Polish Air to Warsaw

Having passed the security at the entrance in Mumbai, I went at stand H for checking in, the line was very long but the good thing was check in was very fast and rapid. Now that was the time me and my aunt were fearing because last time on the Egypt trip, it was where I was rejected from boarding and we got stressed and almost caused some people like my mother a heart attack. I was just on prayers that God should allow me to pass through this stage and I promised everything to God at this moment. When It was my turn, I reached the counter gave my papers, the lady called the manager and asked whether Germany travellers were allowed to board, my heart beat so fast and I started sweating at that moment. After the manager came , he told her it was fine and she then told me that the flight was so loaded and would I like to check in my luggage or no. I told her no because my suit case was a cabin bag. She processed me and I went. At that time I called my aunt and told her I have passed the challenging part, I have my boarding pass and now am heading for emigration. She even lowered her breath and I felt it, as it was heavy. She then told me she was on her knees praying for me to pass these stages. she then told me to rush for emigration and finalise as she wont stop praying till when I am seated waiting for boarding. Before that, I had to Forex all the rupees I had into dollars, the Forex guy also cheated me by ten dollars but I left it because everyone is looking for money. I reached the last check point to emigration or passport control, they checked my bag by x-ray and made me remove everything except the trouser, short and underwear.

Having finished the last security check I had to run to the passport control, one guy was trying to befriend me and asking me questions and I ignored him after answering him with "Good morning but I am not in moods to talk to anyone". He left me and I hurried to the emigration, reaching there, a long queue had manifested and I was almost at the last position. The line was disseminating slowly and it was consuming most of my time yet boarding was in one hour and a half. I waited patiently and till when my turn reached and I submitted my passport, flight boarding passes and covid-19 vaccination certificate. The officer checked them and asked me whether I was a frequent traveller of which I said yes and he took my prints, told me to look in camera and he gave me exit stamp on both passport page and boarding pass. He opened the gate for me to head to the gates for boarding.

I hurriedly went to the gate designated for my flight and waited patiently, after half an hour, they announced boarding and starting with first class, business class and lastly economy class. As always I was in economy class and not premium economy but Pure Economy Class. After the boarding of the Haves we the Haves-not also boarded and the truth was the flight was completely full, congested and compacted. On our way to the aeroplane door, we were given alcoholic cotton sealed towels for sanitisation and the polish beautiful ladies were welcoming us with a sweet grammatical free English voice, "Welcome on board sir/madam, feel conferable and this way sir. My seat was very far Seat 46H and I moved all the way till the middle of the aeroplane and I sat, at the first chair out of the three chairs at H. I love sitting on the window side to observe the beautiful sky and sceneries but this time it was not possible. The plane was big as most international planes are, separated into three columns and each column had tri-chair arrangement with about a 13" – 14" screen and a serving table behind. The chairs were royal-blue in color with white head covers, white pillows and navy blue scurf's. A big and loud audio output where the captain gave information was always like a wake-up alarm in my ears. What amused me was that even male flight attendants were on board and it was my first flight with male attendants. They were good and easy in a sense most males are a little not calm and soft as females. I took my time and observed the inside of the plane comparing it with Emirates, Ethiopian and Egypt air of which I have ever taken flights in. Polish air was also nice and beyond average.I had to call my aunt and inform her that I was soon taking off, she was eagerly waiting for my call like a husband waiting for his wife on the first day of his honeymoon. Having called her and gave her updates, she then decided to take a rest and sleep because it was a huddle for the whole day.

You can have whatever you want.

Having finished boarding, the captain the summoned for take off and we all were requested to tighten our seat belts. I was seated next to two ladies and one next to me was reading a novel and almost finishing it because it was few pages to the end. The other was a young lady about middle twenties and she was taking picture and sending to friends, so I was doing nothing and I just wanted to take a rest due to the huddles I had during the day. Before I switched to aeroplane mode, I sent some people who were caring like Qudus an message that I was in air heading to Poland. We started the take off and as usual that immediate change in altitude always makes everyone feel the weird feeling of instability. After a few minutes, the captain gave us a free will to take off the seat belts and crew started the services. I requested for the earphones and I was given, I loaded a movie because and hoped that I will sleep minus knowing but what led me not to fall asleep was hunger. They started serving from the Haves and it took around an hour. The flight time to destination was about eight hours. When they reached me, they asked me ,"Vegan or non-vegan, I told the lady whether it was possible to get two plates. She laughed yet I was serious, then after I said non-vegan and she served me, chicken, rice, bread, fruits and some adds which I never understood but once I put them in my mouth and they were "Edible I just crushed them. Then after a few minutes, the next crew came with drinks, and they asked the people before me, what they wanted to drink and they told them they could ask for anything like water, juice, beer, wine, tea and coffee. I heard that and put it in my head. Now it was time for me, I said I wanted two glasses of water, one glass of orange juice, one of Apple juice, a cup of tea with milk and one cup of coffee. The ladies next to me were scared and worried, but I never looked at them and I just waited for my order to be served. I was given the things I requested and I started making them disappear.After few minutes I was okay and ready to sleep. I slept for as long as I remember but waking up and we were having more three hours of flight.I decide to watch some movies and I saw another supply of alcoholic towels, I garbed it and wiped my hands and face, then watched my movie again. I saw another serving of eats, it was like maybe I am in a flight but dreaming when I am in a flight and they are serving us foods which they did already. so I was forced to got to the bath-room to see whether I was still sleeping and if I pissing in my pants, the ladies next to me will wake me up. It was not a dream at all, I came back to my seat and they were a almost reaching me. I pretended to have been watching movies and I asked the lady that why was she serving again yet they had just served, she said it was breakfast. I was even smiling in my head, and I just open the serving table and they again gave me eats and asked for the drinks I wanted. I was going to do the same as before but then I stopped on coffee. I really enjoyed the services of this airline and soon after some time the pilot summoned for the descend and soon landing at Warsaw, he announced the seat belt tightening and in about a 30 minutes, we landed at Warsaw. It took around more other twenty minutes before we begun getting off-board and then when we got off board, we had to go to the immigration for entry stamps.

Poland (Warsaw)

Some people were transiting, others were like me who has schengen visa so we never knew where to go and there were many writings in Polish. I asked some ladies who were in front of me whether they might be knowing where people with schengen visa were lining up. The ladies told me they were going in USA so they don't know anything maybe I should try the officers. I asked the officers who were in the security check pints, they told me I was in a wrong line and I was supposed to go by the escalators to the next section because I was not in transit. I was shocked because my tickets were showing that my final destination was Berlin not Warsaw and yet the officer was telling I was not in transit. So I continued as he directed and reached the passport control for entry. As usual lines are always there, but this time it was not a long line. In just a few minutes, I was next to the counter, I handed in my passport which contained the Germany visa, he then asked me some few questions like why I was visiting Germany, any proof documents and whether it was my first time in Europe and many others. I took around five minutes as he was still looking through my documents. After that he gave me back all the documents I had given him and the next thing I heard was a loud sound of his heavy entry stamp head in my passport and he said to me,"Welcome to Europe", the he told me to proceed to the left. At that moment before he stamped my passport while he was screening my documents I was on prayers. I proceeded to the next section. I had a layover of almost one day at Warsaw, I then exchanged my dollars to zloty and I bought some water and chocolate. I was stressed that I was going to sit in the airport for a whole day. So I asked some people whether I was allowed to move out of the airport or not. Because my final destination was Germany and then I was in Poland, so it was like I am still in transit and I cant leave the airport unless I have a transit visa. I then saw an officer and asked him whether I was allowed to move out of the airport and he said yes. He asked me why I was asking and I explained to him. He asked for my passport and looked for the visa, he showed it to me and said I was free to move out and come in any time I wanted because I am in Europe and my visa was enough to travel in almost 26 countries without getting another one. I was surprised and then decided to go out and see how the airport looked like, because I never knew anyone or any place in Poland I could only stop at the airport and because I was fearing that I might be caught outside without Polish visa even though the officer told me, I never wanted to leave the airport premises. I went in again and looked for where I could buy a simcard for single use or timely use. My phone had a fault, it could not connect to WIFI and any other wireless network, so I needed a simcard for communication because I knew my aunt really was in need of updates at the moment because she was the one to update my mother. I bout a simcard around 24xlotys and the lady helped me connect it to network. Immediately I got to network, I got many messages and I had to reply the essential ones at the moment. My aunt was online and I called her on video, I told her I was already in Poland and I was outside the airport, I narrated to her everything as I thought I was till in transit but it seems not, we had a long jazz and she asked for some pictures of the place, airport and even selfies.After the video call, I was then stranded where to go, either I go back inside and sit for the next 29 hours or do the same. My brain was out of options so I decided to go down the airport where I found a train station even though I had seen trains in my country and India but this was more beautiful and organised than what I knew. I did'nt know what I needed to board it, and where to go even so I decided to go back. As I was about to go off the station I decided to ask someone whether they knew anywhere with cheap rooms for rest and refreshing up, they told me but then I told them it was my first time in Poland so I never knew how things worked and I asked him to help me. He agreed and told me that the place was little far in the city and I needed to take a train then I asked him how and he helped me by buying me a one day train ticket and taking me to the place and helping me check in as well then he could leave. It was such a hospitable way I was welcomed by this young man in his early twenties, I entered the train and I was really enjoying the organisation when I reflected back with our trains in Africa and then also compared with the trains in India, this was more of another class which I may say executive. We sat for about 30min and he said it was time to go out. I was just following like a duckling. He then asked me how long I was to stay and what was the maximum amount of money I was to spend on the room in my plans, I told him around 20$, he agreed to take me after searching the nearby place on google maps, we went as he was telling me about his country and himself. He was a good and hospitable person.

City Tour (Warsaw)

Having gotten the room, He helped me check and further asked me whether I was in love with touring the city. I really wanted to but I never had enough money. I asked him how much it would cost because I was not having enough money at the moment, he told me just no amount unless I was going to buy something in the city. I told him whether he can wait and I refresh then we could go. He said he would be back in an hour as his destination was not that far and he was just going to meet some friends of his, so he will let them know that he will not be making it for more time as he was having something to do. I agreed and he left. I took my shower, and change to fresh clothes as I was two days minus change of clothes. I tried to charge my phone and my charger was not European style. After few hours it went off. I was left in the dark and I had not option but to wait for the young man. I took a small nap, and his hard knocks on the door woke me up. I opened for him and he was like sorry he took more time but if I was ready we could go. I agreed and we went out of the motel, went to the bus station pole and waited for the bus, I asked him whether he has ever helped a stranger before the way he helped me and his answer was no because he had never gotten anyone stranger to ask him for help. He was taller than me but phenotypically looked to be younger than me and his shyness were making him talk a lot. He asked me where I was from and where I was heading as usual most conversations where people don't know much about themselves start. The bus arrived at the moment and we boarded, he continued to ask and I was giving answers till when he stopped with his questions and I asked him how old he was when he stuttered I knew he was giving the wrong age, I told him as he looked to be twenty one or two and he said He was. Then he talked about himself more as we continued in the bus and suddenly he said we would start touring from the Old market(Hala Mirowska). We went out and he was showing me many things which were beautiful and if I had money i would buy some but I was not in position to spend till my final destination. He made me tour many places like the Monumental Palace square (World of Wanderlust)in the old town where almost all visitors and tourists go and take picture but my phone was off and I never carried it. He also showed me the graffiti paintings in some places which were really nice and beautiful, the museum which I wanted to enter but tourists and foreigners were to pay some small fees but at them moment I never wanted to spend anything because i never knew what was waiting for me in Berlin. There were beautiful parks, clean and fresh smelling. I had to sit in them because the only way to communicate with nature is by embracing its silence and feeling its purity and beauty from within not by sight. He also sat down with me and I was asking him about life and how he thinks a perfect life one has to live in should be. He was not much into science and life, he openly told me he was a history student and he likes talking about ancient things and past events. Me with history we don't sit on the same table, so I told him I never liked history from day one in high school..I saw the magnificent Palace of culture and science, I wanted to go there but I really was tire and I wanted to sleep, I asked him whether he was okay we go back. We made a tour for about four hours and it was around 8PM and the sun was still in the sky, I was shocked and I could not believe it. It was my first time to see the sun beyond 7PM. We then went back. He brought a conversation and we talk in the bus till when we reached and he helped me see the motel and we entered, I told him that I was very happy and grateful for his hospitable nature and desire to help people. He then told me he will come back in few hours if at all I was okay to have some drink with his friends, they will come and we go. I frankly told him I was not an alcohol person, he suggested a night walk but then I disagreed and I told him I needed sleep since my flight was in the morning tomorrow before 11AM. He agreed and promised to pass by in the morning to show me the way to the airport and I was okay with it. He left and I had to take a nap.

Warsaw to Berlin.

I woke up early in the morning and it was very cold for me as the temperature was around 15 C and I took a warm shower, then opened my laptop and checked for some mails and messages. I used less time because it was the only device I had power on and I still needed it once I reach in Berlin. After a few hours the room service brought Breakfast because it was part of my charges, the only thing they never gave was dinner and lunch as per their terms. I enjoyed it and in a bout one hour my new friend came and he greeted me then asked me the time I was leaving for airport, I told him and he said I still had more time, He started a small jazz and he was talking about what he knows about Africans and I was supplementing even though some were hard facts to accept and others were stereotypes I never wanted to make him angry because he was my only chance to reach the airport and I was trying to fit into his conversation.After some time, I asked him to take me to the airport and he led the way lifting my suitcase good thing I had locked it with a padlock, I was not fearing anything bad to happen. We reached the train station and I though he will leave me and go back but he came with me in the train. I was happy because I never knew which stop I was to go off from. We sat in and he was asking me questions which were personal but because he was the only person I knew and helping me I tried to answer and he was going more deep and I was swimming on top. He wanted to know more about my country, my life, whether I was having someone I loved, whether I have some children and many other things. I was answering and other I was swallowing them and many of them I was slowly giving the answer but in wordy format making it take long for another question as the train moved. we finally reached the train stop to the airport and we went out. He held my bad and made me reach the security line. He finally said good bye and hugged me, with a peck, it made me feel uncomfortable and I looked around to see people's reaction but people were okay and nothing was a big deal. He then waved and said to me loudly as it was nice to meet me and I should have a safe journey and maybe next time I should visit Poland again for many adventures. I was like sweating in and out but had to stay "Dry" to fit in the society. I then said to him back as I was grateful and happy to meet him. The lady before me told me as that was how most love stories begin and how most of them end as well. She went further and asked me how long I had known him because we seemed to be loving each other so much. I got angry and I was to react badly to the old lady but then I told her the truth that he was just a friend whom I had met and he helped me in many things yet I never knew him. She said then I must keep such people in life and maybe the next time I visit Poland I may need him of which she was right and unlucky my phone was off and I never took his contacts except he had connected with me on Instagram. We checked in and I went to gate 33 to wait for my flight. We boarded and the flight time was so short about 2hours. In the flight I met these two young boys who were going to Berlin for vacation and they were all talkative and one was in the front the other in the my seat section. Since it was a local flight we used smaller plane, it was a two column plane with two seats per column. As always when I sit with anyone I just greet them and that's all. The young boys in their teenage age looked to be from fancy homes, so when I greeted the one next to me, they both answered and they all started to ask me the Usual questions and I was happy to answer as always. But the good thing was these boys wanted to know more about Africa and they were just fascinated by the way Africa is talked about, by their parents because one of them told me as their parents were once doctors in South Africa. I decided to beautify my continent more and the credited my country more in the eyes of these teenagers. I talked with them for quite a long time and they were happy to also get a clear picture of Africa from the native person. Having landed at Berlin, I thought I had to go in passport control but the officer I met told me that, I was already in Europe I needed not any more stamps whether I get it from Netherlands or Poland or Finland what ever European country I get the entry stamp from, it was enough.I was so mesmerised by the beauty of Berlin airport and moreover I was in the local flight's section. I went down stairs and I was in the train station. This was so beautiful for me and I was so surprised by everything. I had to purchase a 9 euro ticket for public transport, it was a ticket valid for three months from June to end of August which allowed free access to public transport all over Germany no matter what the distance was. I tried the vending machines along the train station, one lady I met directed me where I could but one and I was in hurry to do there. Now all these were setting me for another journey full of memories to Greifswald. I went and purchased the ticket and asked the officer I met, where I could get the next train to Greifswald. He pulled out the train system and movement locator and directed me to the station. He told me it was to leave in about 10min I rushed and sloped the stairs and reached the train station, I saw an African guy and I was like seeing a saviour. I went to him and talked with him.

CHAPTER FOUR

Germany (Berlin to Greifswald).

The African guy I met was so calm and hospitable that he gave me time and I explained to him where I was going and he decided to help me. But how did I start the conversation with him and even how did I know he spoke English even he was African or German but black? First when he saw me, he winked at me and that alone showed me that he was an African and with English I saw his phone was in English when he was sending a message because we well all standing at the same train station. Now when he winked, I disappeared in crown because I was fearing being scammed and pick pocketing so I pass very far and reached him then observed the language he was using on his phone once I saw it was English, I went nearest to him and I said "Hello" to him.I asked him whether he could help me to navigate my way to Greifswald and he also never knew because it was very far from Berlin. He told me to download DB-navigator app but my phone was down and secondly I never bought sim card at the airport. He checked the train connections I had to take and told me he will leave me at the last main train station which goes inter-states in Germany because where I was heading it was in a different state. After some few minutes, the train we were waiting for arrived and he told me to board. I sat and I asked him where the ticket I had was able to work in the train I was in. He look at it and told me it was okay. He then told me more about the 9e ticket and how it works, which trains and buses I can take with it and all other things. He told me his name but I am poor at remembering people's names unless I live with them for a while. So we sat in train for around 30min and he told me I was supposed to go to Berlin Hauptbahnhof. But then I told him, as it was my first time in Germany and Europe as well, so he decided to led me to the Berlin Hauptbahnhof station which was a 10min walk.I didn't have much to talk with him because I was feeling cold and I was exhausted. when we reached Berlin Hauptbahnhof, he checked the app and told me as the next train I was to take leaves in 20min, we entered the building and he told me to take a write down of the places I will pass through before leaving the train, I wrote them down and then he left. I was thankful to him and he told me I was welcome in Germany. That same day was the start date of my program in Germany "Sustain MV" of which I missed the first day as I was still in travel. Before I left Poland, I had made a communication to the organising team and the members who were attending the program about my travels so they were all aware, and I never had to worry. Reaching the Berlin Hauptbahnhof I had to wait for about 20min for the train to arrive and we board.

Glance at Berlin Hauptbahnhof

What catches one's eye is the big Cuboid Glass building to which a big text Berlin Hauptbahnhof is written, en-carved in glass with a white color and a clock beneath it, at the sides many tall glass building and in the far front the beautiful bridge road which give a good view. Just a little far from the glass buildings are the state of the art hotels with beautiful sculpture on their walls and after the bridge, a beautiful green park with many light stands. Below the bride is a flowing stream of water to which many ferries and expensive boats are rod. The ferries carry tourists and natives along the stream looking at the beautiful view of the city. Just outside the Berlin Hauptbahnhof building, the roads which are interconnected make the crowd and the Berlin Hauptbahnhof be intense and people of different talents just showcase them along side the roads.

Inside the Berlin Hauptbahnhof, there are beautiful big screen showing the different train schedules, and types of trains.Many escalators run in opposite directions from different levels of the Berlin Hauptbahnhof building. The building seemed to have more than four levels and inside were beautiful shops of different things. Security and information desks were at every corner to maintain order and organisation. Last but not least of the Berlin Hauptbahnhof was the crystal clear audio-speakers which were giving enough ambient sound with stops once announcements were to be delivered. With those few things I observed about Berlin Hauptbahnhof it was time to board my train to Greifswald. Before boarding I met a man in his late 20s and he started a conversation with me, as always he was asking me where I was heading and little did I know he was going in the same place as me, I talked with him and he was telling me about his college life and his research work. I was so touched and excited by his research work and his desire to make a better life and improve digital security and privacy. Having entered the train, I managed to get a seat at the first level where I was seeing everything. The man I entered with decide to sit a little far from me because he first secure for me a sit and on securing his, it was very far from mine.

Greifswald here I come

In a few minutes, the train started to move. There were many teenagers in the section I sat who later I knew were going for summer camping but little did I know that they were going to the same Hotel I was heading too. They were very many and as you know they were in their country, they never feared to speak or do anything they wanted, and I also did not know any rules in Germany so I was seeing everything new. The journey was for about 4hrs and many stops were there if I estimate them, they were around 8 stops to 10. I was really hungry, exhausted and I was not in moods to talk to anyone. I saw one boy with a free charger which I predicted to fit in my phone, then I removed my charger and phone and I asked some of them whether I could charge in the train, one boy came and showed me where the power output was but I knew he would try to help me place it inside and so he did. When he tried it and it could not fit in, he immediately called his friend whom I saw with the same charge to help me, the my phone was plunged in and started charging. I could not bother to power it on because the most important thing was not working at the time, that was Internet because I had not sim card and "Remember my phone doesn't connect to wireless connections". so I had to just charge it and maybe take a few picture and that's all. After a while the boy sitting next to me left the sit on a particular station, there was free sit, a small young but silent boy sat next to me after a while. I knew he wanted to talk to me but he was nervous and was shy. I greeted him first and he replied. He could not make a mature conversation but rather asking me some small questions and he was out of words. I decide to then create one. On the way we passed via a large field of wind mills and I wanted to know more about them but I couldn't ask anyone. So I asked him and he told me many things about the wind mills and how his father is an engineer in the energy company and they keep repairing them and he has climbed it more than once. I saw that the only was to make the boy talk to me was for me to show him that I was new and I never knew anything about Germany an d where we were going. So he decided to talk to me and telling me things he knew about each point we passed through and I asked him any questions. After a while their coordinator came and told them as they were to get off in at the next station and little did I know that there was a screen showing the stations and so I observed because the young boy had told me. The PA-system in the train was available but speaking in German, so I was counting of the exit of the man I entered with but in the few talks I had with the boy, the guy had left at a stop before and it was having Greifswald but with another word, yet mine was Greifswald alone. Then the boys were getting off at Greifswald and I also had to get off. I got off and decided to follow the teenagers where they went because I expected to atleast meet some elder people and ask them. The first impression I got was the many bikes and bikers in Greifswald. I went to the bus station and passed by the teenagers and I heard one of them telling a friend in "English" and I knew she used "English" because she wanted me to hear what she was saying, she said to her friend that it seemed that their summer camp was hosting some people from other countries besides Germany and Europe at large. I went and asked the lady next to the station whether she knew the next bus to Wieck and she told me it was in the next few minutes.

Majuwi Greifswald

Majuwi is a short form for Maritimes Jugenddorf Wieck and this was my first accommodation in Germany. When I sat in the bus from the station, I did not know after how many stops I should leave the bus because I had no communication from anyone. I just waited till when all the people I boarded with came out from, and I also came out with hope that I will ask anyone I could meet most especially those who knew English. I just enjoyed looking outside the bus windows seeing children and adults riding bicycles. At the last stop, the bus stopped and I was the last person to get out, before I was out I showed the drive the paper containing my address and he just pointed in front. I was now knowing where to go but blind folded that I did not know where exactly I was supposed to stop. The teenagers I came with moved and left me. I walked for about 5min and I decided to stop, Looking in sides I saw a local bar, I went to ask whether anyone could help me with direction, they just looked at me and ignored. I continued a little further and I saw a lady holding a baby by her arms, I decided to try her and when I showed her the direction to where I was heading she lead the way, I followed. She never knew English and was communicating in German of which I was not understanding but kept on nodding my head. When she reached me at the hotel, she showed me where to find the reception and then she left, I just accepted and thanked her in an Indian way of shaking my head with a smile and she went further. On entering the reception area, there was a man in his middle 30s whom I asked whether he could understand English and he acknowledged, I then showed him a paper containing my accommodation address and asked him whether I was at the correct place. He said it was the correct place, for confirmation I asked him the second time and then he also asked me whether I was part of the Sustain MV team of which I said yes. He got a paper to which all the attendees of the program were printed and their room allotment, I showed him my name and he asked me whether I had any contact with the coordinator of the program such that he could confirm before he could allow me in the room. I remembered that my phone had been charged and it contained mails which had communication information for Carmen and Elisabeth who were the coordinators.

I gave him the contacts and on the first try they never picked but trying the second time, they picked and talked till when Elisabeth asked me on phone and I talked with her, she then told me to hand over the phone to the person at the reception. After talking, the man told me to wait a little at the waiting area as the room needed some small service like five to ten minutes, he would call me once its done. I agreed and went outside instead of the waiting area. On reaching, I met all the teenagers I was with right from the train to the bus and now at the same accommodation area. I was surprised and I went and sat in the sun because I was feeling cold as the temperatures were low for me compared to India's temperature which I was used to. After some time, the receptionist came looking for me and could not find me at the waiting area, till when he asked someone and I saw one boy pointing at me when he saw me. He led me to the room and opened it, I noticed one thing in Germany all their doors and windows opened moving inside which was really hard for me to master at that short time. I entered the room, and I observed it first, felt the freshness and held at the sheets and blanket. I first got my luggage at the bed, opened it and took out the essentials I needed at the time, things like took brush, paste, cream, bathing soap and fresh clothes. I entered the bath room to take a shower after a long day, the bathroom was super crystal clean with beautiful full clear mirrors and other incentives like shampoo, room freshener and other things I never knew. I switched on the water and it was ice cold, I almost cried in the bathroom, I had been used to India's temperature where we don't use hot water switched and I had forgotten that it was Europe where they warm the houses instead of cooling them. I looked for the warm water switch, then I took a good shower and the towels were pure white, scented and fluffy that it was so relaxing on my skin. I went out of the bathroom, wore my clothes and I checked my phone to see what time it was, and my phone was showing 7PM yet the sun was so bright and it seemed to be like 5PM so I thought my phone was not updated and I had to leave it alone. I entered the bed and decided to take a nap before my friends who were for the day 1 event could come back and maybe I interact with them at night. The bed was so big that I nearly felt like it was making me feel uncomfortable, the blanket was so soft, dense and white with all the bed coverings and the pillow. I was in fear of not making them dirty because I am not a person of white. I was feeling fresh and smelling fresh that I felt asleep in minutes and yet it was still daytime.

Having taken a nap for about three to four hours, I woke up and I was surprised to still see the sun but this time it was just setting. I heard some of the people speaking about how that day's lecture was good and they also talked about how there was a new guy who arrived and so they were heading to my room. Alex was one of the persons who was very friendly, welcoming and likeable in the sense that he would fit in anyone's character, he came to my room and talked with me. He was the first person I talked with and he told me as they were going to have some beers outside maybe I could join them. I told him I was not a person of drinking, and he told me to just go and interact with them. After a while I heard people talking about one more other lady who had also just arrived called Setara and never did I know that she was the lady I was chatting with on WhatsApp when I was coming and we had promised to meet each other at the Berlin train station which never happened because I lost connection and I could not contact her any more. The evening was so as being my first interaction with the team and amidst the night as people were drinking and I and Setara were eating apples because she was a Muslim and could also not join the party of drinking, bees started to sting some people i think it was due to the beer flavour and sugar but I was surprised of bees who move at night so we decided to leave the pier were we were having the evening time and moved into our rooms. Many people were exhausted at that time and had to go and sleep while a few remained and went to Alex's room and continued the drinking party. I was joined them to get the interaction and vibe for a few hours till when I was being cracked by sleep and fall off.

CHAPTER FIVE

Sustain MV 1

Since I had spent one extra day in travel, I missed the opening day of Sustain MV and thus my program started on the second day. In the morning having taken my shower, I was directed to the cafeteria where breakfast was served at the hotel where we had our first accommodation.I moved out holding my coat in m hands, reaching out the weather was so cold for me because I had not been used to it and yet others were okay with it as most people were wearing short clothes and light clothes. When I went to the cafeteria I looked around to see whether I can understand how the system worked. It was very different from something I knew and I had to ask someone. I saw a young man whom I did not know was part of our team and he told me how things worked. The services of this cafeteria were very good in organisation, it was like something I had seen once in Egypt. All fruits were rounded at a particular place in bowls some where whole fruits while others were cut fruits placed in smaller portions. There were many fruits like apples in different colors, peas, pineapples and guavas with many others whose names I did not know and a few were my first sight on them. The tea and coffee section was separated with many coffee and tea machines which were automated, the unlucky part I had was cold milk. In my country and even in India we are used to hot milk on breakfast with cork-flakes and other things but I got a new experience of cold milk breakfast. The bread section was the most beautiful and most decorated one with many different bread types made from different things and impregnated with stuff like peanuts, groundnut, sunflower seed and plains also. Many spreading items like margarines, chocolate, jams of different colors and cheese in different types were all present. The cups and plates were made up of ceramic or fortified clay and white in color with many different cutlery ranging from small to large spoons, forks, knives and sticks. The tables were perfectly curved in wood and with locally made napkins and wood mats which we were putting our food stuff on. I got some milk, apples, bread, egg, chocolate and hot black tea and I took. At that moment I saw an African guy, I approached his table wit a few of his friends and I sat, before I started eating one of his friends who was a Ph.D scholar in London asked me in a very familiar way and he knew my name even. So I was surprised and little did I know that I was chatting with him too during the travel time. They all introduced themselves to me and I was so happy that the African guy was from a country next to mine "Rwanda" so we had to be brothers at that time. In a short while as we were still jazzing, I heard one mature man in his 30s saying that we should harry up as the next but to Greifswald was in ten minutes, I asked the people I was with who he was, they all told me his name was FRANK one of the coordinators of Sustain MV. We then hurried and finished out breakfast, in that same cafeteria was the group of teenagers I came with the day before and were not part of our team but had hotel reservation in the same hotel. After about ten minutes I followed the new friends I had made at the instant. We then met Elisabeth and Frank at the pier and proceeded to the bus stop.In around five minutes the bus arrived and we boarded, using our 9eticket to Greifswald University.It took around ten minutes to reach, I was mesmerised at the magnificent building of this University and their architecture which I will describe later in my own way.

A trek through Greifswald University

Having reached Greifswald University, we moved around looking for the seminar hall where we were to have a lecture on

"Sustainability and how it is being implemented in Greifswald to attain carbon Neutrality by 2030". The buildings were very beautiful, ancient like for the early 50s, they were all having sculpture which were en-curved in marble and black quartz. They were also prominent in a sense that each building was individually distinct from each other with magnificent feature like doors, old calligraphic wordings and symbols of majesty and power. The floor of the whole University was tiled with sea stones which were having no distinct pattern but just to make the place dust free and beautiful. Along each building was a given symbol and wording which indicated the title of the building and the significance it had to the University. The University had a big church located almost to the end of the old market, the church had a monastery all these were prominent structure and beautiful mega old structures which were in their innate stage and never demolished or intact but just renovated for reinforcement to overcome heavy winds and storms. We were to have our lecture on the small computerised hall but due to COVID-19 fears, we had to use the main big hall. We moved slowly to the hall, and upon entry of the hall is the beautiful en-curved door, black in color with silver and gold coatings on the door knobs,and linings i think to prevent corrosion and maintain the beauty of the place. The hall was graduated to the third floor and we had to take the stair or elevator for those who wanted, this time Elisabeth was leading by the stairs. We entered and the stairs were all tiles in a given pattern and gold-brown lined, marble and quartz crystals were placed at the walls of the building and very fine sorted wood was used for the stair handles. Beautiful ancient paintings were fixed in the corridors of each level of the hall, good crystal chandeliers were fixed in the middle of the corridors with small leaf petals like-lighting on each picture frame which illuminated them. The whole building was fitted with heat delivery pipes which ran through all the building delivering heat during heavy freezing winters and finally we had reached the hall. Upon entry Elisabeth was welcomed by the professor who was to take us through the lecture and we all entered. I looked at the whole building and started to stare at every piece of technology, artefact, art and furniture which was placed in the hall. The immediate attention was taken by the sitting system which allowed each individual to sit without disturbing the other, this was very amusing because normally when we sat in halls that I used to visit, when one sits and leaves and empty sit and another person wants to sit on it, they have to stand up and even walk from their sit allowing the person to sit first, this was not the case as each sit was independent of the other with its own writing pad. Upon sitting, we were given five minutes to settle before the start of the lecture, I looked around and saw many knobs of which seemed to be like clothes hangers but fitted in the walls, some were immediately after the entrance and others were behind the hall wall. I asked the German person next to me what would be the use of the knobs I was seeing and he told me they were for hanging coats, jackets, heavy clothes in case one comes with them most especial;y during winter season. I asked him, why would they remove their warming clothes and hang them during winter yet its very freezing times, he looked at me and asked where I was from, I felt insulted but he was right I was never in a country where it falls snow and temperatures below zero. I told him I was from India and he nodded his head in a way of saying I did not know for sure I had to ask, He then told me that the white lined pipes that ran through the whole building were heating coils which are switched on during winter and provide heat in the whole building making the temperature favourable. I kept on looking at the whole building inside where we were sitting to see things I can narrate and write into my books but all were new to me. The hall had big screen which were connected a computers and a huge camera which was for recording all the activities, whether plays, lectures, movies and other things that took place in the hall. In a short time, the lecture started, delivered by a professor in his late 50s, he talked about the beauty of the planet, the need to conserve it and our role to play as youths in this campaign. He also taught us how to calculate our own carbon footprints and explained the significance of being responsible as a species on earth and on of the reasons he gave for the need to be responsible, accountable and curious about climate change and climate deterioration activities was, we have only one earth and once we break it down we will have no home. After a few hours of the lecture it was lunch time and we had to visit the lunch points in the institute.

My first taste of German food.

At this point I had not memorized the names of some of the people in the program so, I was just following them. We moved towards the cafeteria, hovering through the University again I saw many infrastructures, statues and beautiful flowers along side houses. We reached the cafeteria and my first impression was the way things were organised inside with automated systems which allowed making orders in less time and this reduced the waiting time and crowd in the place. The unfortunate bit was every single word in this place was in German language and it was hard to understand which foods to pick and which not to take. The challenge was I am not supposed to eat some foods, and some ingredients when used in the preparation of foods. I had to ask people what they were taking and one friend helped interpret the menu. I really never knew what to take because all the foods were new to me except French fries and ketchup. So for the first time, I ordered the fries and some water. My first meal in Germany was really not very good because of the restrictions I have on my diet which literally inhibits me from eating certain foods especially meat unless some conditions are fulfilled and drinks as well. I took the fries and ketchup with water. My lunch as over, I waited for my friends to finish up and then we can go to the next program. I will not tell you that we ever came back to this cafeteria again till I left Germany but it was a beautiful place. The arrangement of all the furniture and the services were at 4 star level as students were so organised and no one cared about what or who was entering or leaving the cafeteria. beautiful fumes were masked in the place to give a good scent and relaxing German music was played in the background, the lights were yellow day light making the place always welcoming and the tables were attractively designed to allow moments of nice meals making it a better place to relax and forget a little about the stress from the lecture hall. I never tested whether it had free WiFi because my phone could not connect to wireless connections. We moved out of it and went down to the monument where we had to meet Elisabeth, Carmen and Frank for the next program. As promised, Carmen gave me back the 100ethat we paid as application fees, at the monument place. The monument had a long black marble statue which looked to be old and just a few meters from it was a small pool of water which contained small fountains and these made a beautiful view as children used to play in. At this time, the bus was waiting for us to take us on another amusing journey of adventure and learning. Elisabeth was already at the bus and Frank was with us coming. Soon as we reached the bus, we entered and we started the ride.

The Afternoon and evening of that day.

We drove for about one hour to one and half hour, during the course of the ride, we passed in a field of many wind mills and these were about 100to200 in number. On reaching the final stop, we were assembled at a small station which was the center for Hydrogen and Wind energy project in Mecklenburg- Western Pomerania. Frank at this juncture was the coordinator present while Elisabeth and Carmen were busy with other duties. We waited for the professors who were in-charge of the project to arrive. After a few minutes, they arrived and we got addressed and split into two groups; one which would start with the Hydrogen car exhibition and the other which would start with the Hydrogen plant exhibition. I was in the Hydrogen Plant exhibition.

The Wind and Hydrogen Plant Tour.

We followed the professor to the plant, which contained machines that carried out water splitting using electricity a process scientifically known as electrolysis. The professor explained the process and in his explanation he mentioned how the two products obtained during water break down (Oxygen and Hydrogen) are obtained. The process included things like separation of hydrogen from oxygen, purification of hydrogen and storage of hydrogen. at that juncture we asked him where the oxygen goes during the process and he said it was released in the atmosphere which asked whether they could not also harness it and use it as it was also valuable. His reaction to the question was that the required purity of oxygen for hospital and fuel usage was very high which required more sophisticated machines to purify incurring more expenses, thus releasing it in the atmosphere was the best solution as its not a harmful gas to the environment. After showing us how hydrogen was made and stored under high pressure in heavy steel metal canisters, he took us to the next plant which was for the generation of electricity from hydrogen as green energy. In the plant were heavy engines which burnt hydrogen producing high temperatures which were used to drive the motors in the engine to produce energy and also heating the buildings and houses during winter seasons while releasing water as a by-product. As the tour for the Hydrogen plant ended, we had to go back and check on the hydrogen powered car as the next group went in. The car features were as for the normal modern cars except that it was using green energy (Hydrogen), fuelfells and producing no toxic by-products to the environment. After a few minutes we went to the Wind mill plant field where we visited and got an chance to enter on the mills and also got to know how it works and how it was constructed. the mill was about 200meters high or more with very big base almost size of a self contained house, with an entrance door and above it were blades which were very long, aerodynamically shaped to reduce wind resistance, they were about 10to20meters long, the knot at which the blades were fixed was huge about the size of a single double bed room, housing the motor which rotated to produced energy in form of DC. Inside the mill was a huge connection of wires from the top of the mill knot to a series of generators which were used to transform the DC current to the AC and them step it up which was then supplied to the different users. The professor explained how green the process was in a way that once the winds blow so high that too much energy is produced by the wind plant, because they do not have cells or batteries that can 100% store the energy minus losses, they use the excess energy to split water into hydrogen which can then be kept and once need it required for energy it can be combusted and energy is produced. The method ensures almost effective energy supply and demands can be met.

After the long day, we finished the program and took some picture then headed back to the accommodation. On reaching Greifswald, we were exhausted but people passed at the supermarket and bought some drinks for the night while I was just in the wagon. We reached accommodation and I had to take shower due to the long day but one lady brought a suggestion of waiting for the sunset at the pier and take pictures. I was about to disagree but then I told myself why would I deny to experience something provided that it was not dangerous, then I joined the picture party. During the picture capture I asked what time the sunset normally happens in Europe, because I had looked at my phone and it was showing a half passed eight in the evening which shocked me. Most of the people who were from Europe told me that it sets very late in the summers at around nine to ten in the evening. I thought India was weird were it sets at around a half passed five in the evening but I was surprised to hear and also witness by my eyes when it was around a quarter to ten in the evening when the sun was still in the sky. After the pictures I got to my room and refreshed then prepared to sleep. In a about one hour, a friend knocked my door and asked me whether I would join them at the sea, they were going to spend a night there drinking, dancing, swimming and doing all the crazy stuff. I was to reject because I don't drink, before I said no he told me I could buy myself a soda in the vending machine and join them since I don't drink alcohol. I agreed and wore my heavy sweater and told him to meet him in five minutes. It was very cold weather for me as for them, it was good weather. The coldness almost penetrated all the wearing I had and reached my skin and bones. But most people were wearing very light clothes and even were having the guts to swim in the freezy cold sea water.

The night at the sea.

As we approached to go to the sea, one of our friends who was the last to come arrived and we had to get him to his room, we got hold of his luggage and lifted it to his room, then Alex, the friend who had called me to join them at the sea also persuaded the new guy to join us. As we were to the beach, the other friend also joined. We reached the beach and many people were there, the teenagers of which I had come with last time and then our group. Music, dancing and other things were taking place. I was literally bored because my personality doesn't enjoy partying and loud noise. So I drunk my Fanta, slowly as I was watching and feeling the cold in my bones. After some few minutes, one guy came and started a conversation with me of which it was a good one. We talked about politics, and then shifted to science by the time we finished and I was feeling so cold that my bones could not handle the cold we were talking about the minority groups of the LGBTQ+ community and he was elaborating more about the need for equality and justice among all. After a while a friend from Rwanda also was tired and wanted to sleep. Once I heard him asking whether someone was in need of going to sleep, I just cancelled the conversation more over I had nothing to contribute in the conversation. So we went back to the accommodation and on the way we got lost and decided to pass through the plantations. We met a wire fence and it was just the only thing we had to jump and get to the place we had our rooms. I jumped successfully but my friend was drunk and on jumping he was pierced by the wire in his foot. It was really not a good thing because the day next we had a lot of tours and lecturers. As we went back to the rooms, I just ran into bed and covered myself with many blankets to get myself warm. The next day, as usual we went for breakfast and Alex with his friends who had stayed till around three in the morning were late for the breakfast and he did not take it that day because the bus was leaving by the time he was from his room.

The Day In Rostock

We drove for almost two hours and finally we had reached the University of Roctock. The city of Rostock was not more than the Greifswald, we started our day at the Bioprocessing Lab where we had a tour and lecture on how garbage in Germany most in the region was collected,sorted and then transformed into biofuel, and biogas for university consumption. We toured the lab and observed the instruments which were used in the processing of garbage to energy. One thing I noticed was in Germany garbage sorting was common with color coated bins with labels demacating the type of garbage to be dropped in and some machines which gave back some token when specific type of garbage is dropped in. We then headed to the Albert Einstein Lab which was a few minutes walk away from the first point of entry into Rostock University. Here we had a lecture about Performing Chemistry with The sun. The lecture was looking at the different ways in which sun energy can be harnessed and used as a driving factor for chemistry in the industries to reduce the burning of coal and fossils. The lecture hall was so beautiful, computerised and we had a very good interaction with the professor who showed us the level at which her research was reached. After some few hours we went for lunch and as usual the cafeteria are always nice and having a variety of dishes. This cafeteria was the first I had seen with rice and other foods and I really enjoyed the lunch. We then went into another lecture of Sustainability but this time from a Social Science professor. I will be honest this was the lecture that I never enjoyed because it was just about talking and no practical knowledge and application. After around two hours we had to take a City tour and I was exited.

The City Tour.

Having finished the boring lecture, We were all exited for the city tour. This time Frank was the tour guide and at this time we were told to tour any place we wanted provided that we could make it back to the next point of meeting. I was so exited and I saw it as a chance to grab myself a sim card and connect back to media and call back home as well. I asked one of my friends who knew German to help me but he was very busy with his new girl and I noticed that I was making him uncomfortable so I left the sim card issue. We all followed Frank who showed us the different monumental and historical artefacts in University of Rostock, these included great gigantic churches, museums and monasteries. He further showed us the wall of Rostock which was build to protect it again invaders and we further went to the great building of the university which was looking so beautiful and Gold coloured with different heroes or priests who were believed to have been great. Just a few slops away from the building was a musical magical event and we stood there for a while to observed the beautiful performances and observe the culture as well. We then continued and went to the main church building which Frank told us was more than 300years old and it ceased to be a worshipping church at the moment but rather a used for initiation ceremonies of freshers and convocations. As most cities we toured in Germany, Rostock also had its own Market but this time they were two the new market and the old market. All these were having beautiful materials to buy and memorial pendants and amulets. We moved till we reached the University again and we were heading in for the next program which was about the music and drama program from the University of Rostock.

HMT program and Concert

We reached at the School of Music, filming and drama. We were told to do rapid antigen test for COVID-19 while some people had done the test early in the morning, some of us like me, never did because I was lacking connection to get the updates from the group. I was given the test kit to test myself. After some few minutes, we were allowed inside the campus and we were mesmerised by the beauty of the place with many picture of successful artists who had passed through the college. The instructor came and we interacted with him, toured the theatre. The theatre was so big in comparison to the theatres of schools I have been before, it was sound and light proofed with many speakers and lights. We went inside and took some pictures and made noise as well. It was really fan and inspiring for those who were in the love of music and drama. We also went to one of the lecture rooms which was o good, and we sat in a circular format as the instructor played for us some music notes from the piano. I saw many music instruments and I was really happy to see the joy of people who understand and treasure music. The instructor told us that people study and get to graduate with qualification in music. I asked him the type of music he was talking about and he told me that music which is cooperate and calming like Oprah. Then I understood what he meant because many people in the world with not even a certificate have gone to the entertainment sector. He then took us through a lecture of How Sustainability can be integrated into the entertainment sector . It was a very live and informative discussion because he showed us some of the projects made by his students to ensure sustainable music delivery and conservation of the music to the next coming generations and the present. We had a good time with the instructor and really I enjoyed his perspective of music because it was so positive that it gave much insight of what melodious and sweet music can and how it can really promote ones life and experiences. After, we went for the pizza because we were so exhausted and hungry.

During the pizza time I had a small discussion with some few people about women equity and involvement in decision making. It was a healthy discussion and I enjoyed it which made me grasp their perspective and understood their point of view as women and how they feel when most things are having more percentages to men. In a few minutes we were directed to the concert hall where some Master's students were going to give their last presentations in Music and Singing. In the hall besides us from the SustainMV summer school, majority of the people were elderly men and women. All masks on and social distancing we sat and the concert started. German was the language of usage and I will be honest even 2% was much in the things I understood. I though it would be like these concerts where big drums, loud noise, and many instruments to my surprise a well dressed gentleman in his late 50s came in with his tabled and sat on a piano, then after a few seconds a well dressed beautiful lady in her early 30s came and soon before the start, the master of ceremony had talked and people were anxious waiting and in about a few seconds the first piece of the piano note was tapped. I looked at the elderly people shaking their heads and looking at each other. after a few notes being played, the lady shouted in a very loud and masculine voice, I almost felt into laughter but them remembered Oprah music is always like that. It was like she was following the tones of the piano and different notes she was to sing in maybe tanner, soprano, base and others. Finally the concert was about to end when the master of ceremony also sang which was really unexpected because based on how he looked, he had a belly, generally fat and no one expected him to have the lungs and vocals for the Oprah singing, he sang both in German and English and its the only song I got to understand and then really accepted that sometimes talent is not what we need but belief and once one believes in themselves then Hope sets in and eventually they will do anything. The day was very nice and we ended it so beautifully

and we went to our bus to going back to Greifswald. We drove
back and most people like me had got tired and we just looked for
our rooms to sleep though some other people were still having
some programs. The day ended for me and soon as I entered I
took a shower and entered the bed.

CHAPTER SIX

Sustain MV 2

It was again another day full of excitement and as usual we get our breakfast and then head to the bus stop, but this time it was different. It was Checking-out day we had to leave Greifswald for Stralsund. Elisabeth told us to pack our belongings and we checkout in the morning but before we head for Straslund, we had to first go for the Pit-land excursion program so we hurried to pack and checkout officially but we go a secure room to keep our things which we would pick after the excursion. Having done so and taken breakfast, we headed to the bus stop and in less than ten minutes we boarded and headed over to the pit-lands. We met our guide then Elisabeth introduced us and she left for her official duty at the University, Frank and Us stayed for the program. The lady made a good introduction and explained to us what pit-lands were and how important they were in carbon sequestration and carbon sinks. She also showed us the maps showing different pit-lands in Germany and how many have been destroyed due to construction and others due to farming and animal grazing. After a few minutes, she showed us tools which we were to go with for the excursion and asked volunteers to carry them, there was a harmer of which I volunteered to carry and drilling metals which were carried by someone else. It was very sunny and people were creaming their bodies with sunscreen, as usual African bodies, no need for sun shield. We went deep into the water logged fields and the instructor gave us more insights about the pit lands and we started drilling. I made the first drill and she continued to teach us the profile of the pit-land and how decomposition mechanisms can be analysed using the soil sections. We enjoyed the excursion and she ate some of the soils from the drill hoe showing how safe they are and by doing so she can detect the levels of water in the pit-land. Other people also tried the same but I did not because it was smelling really not nice. She also made us to dig one more hole and this time people looked for a new site that seemed to be untouched.After a few minutes it was ended and we had to go for lunch and also set off for Stralsund.

Last hours in Greifswald.

This time everyone had the liberty to find themselves where to eat and what to eat, I tried following a few people but once they settled at a place where I saw I could not be comfy I left them and moved my way, till when I met Setara in the old market when she was looking at some clothes and I told her to keep around such that I can look for somewhere to buy a sim card. I started scanning each corner of the market looking for the sim shop, they were very many like Oxygen, Vodafone, etc. but the former was so expensive about 40ewhile the later was not easy to get and so the only sim shop for Vodafone was hidden and I had to move and scan. When I failed to get it, I went to the tourist center where I met some few teenagers whom I asked help from and one of them showed me the map and decided to take me to the shop. The boy was so talkative but because I was the one in need I had to give him my attention and he was talking about himself and telling me about the city of Greifswald and many things till when the worst part came when he started asking about me. I had no option but rather to answer all the questions he had for me. He was just a young teenage and curious to know because they normally receive less African tourists in Greifswald. Once we reached the shop, he talked and I was given the sim card costing around 14ewhich I was okay with. The boy decided to pay it because I had 50eas the least amount in my pocket. I told him we should get change and I pay him back, he refused and was like it was a favour of good heart. He then took my new number and Instagram contact. But I then told him as I was leaving the town soon for Stralsund and it was nice meeting him. He looked worried and said we would meet again once and maybe he will call me some day which I agreed. Having gotten the sim card I was told to wait for about an hour and I will activate it in my phone. I then hurriedly looked for Setara or anyone who by any chance is in the program. I walked here and there seeing no one till when I saw Setara passing by on video call with her family the I decided to follow. After few minutes she told she was going to have lunch then go to the bus station back to Wieck, I just told her I was lost so we should go together. She agreed and we went to the cafeteria for lunch but because the bus was almost reaching the station, we had to take a take away then rush to the bus stop. We reached to the stop and the bus was about 10 minutes to the station, so we waited and for Setara, she never waited for reaching the accommodation to eat, she started at the waiting station. A few minutes later some people also from the program joined us at the waiting and we boarded back together. Reaching the place, we were the latest to arrive and many people had secured their luggage but I had to eat first and more importantly I had to insert in my new sim card. I did and entered the activation pin, it worked and many messages from social media started pouring in. In a few minutes we were to leave yet I had to first eat my lunch. I ate with no pressure and slowly because it was my favourite chicken and chips. My luggage was the last to be removed from the secure room. When I finished eating I took my luggage to the bus and entered. At that time Frank was to go to Stralsund by bike so he left before us. Having sat in the bus, I look at the place and I was really going to miss it because I was almost starting to understand it and even enjoying the people and the environment. We drove for a very long time about 4 hours and we reached Stalsund.

Stralsund

The beautiful harbour with many ships, Yacht, ferries and boats which roam around the city waters gives the impressive view of Stralsund. On off-boarding the bus, we were asked to leave our luggage and it will be delivered to our places of stay once we reach there. In a few minutes we go new coordinators who were stationed in Stralsund and they handed us a small package in a red bag. In the bag were the requirements we were to use and the keys to our rooms. We then had a small tour of the area headed by the senior tour guide in the place. This was the basis for all the events of SustainMV till the end of the program. As most cities in Germany have churches same was Stralsund and markets as well. Many historical buildings and City gates were there. The harbour was the most tourist attraction point of this place as it hosted many beautiful boats, sailors and Ferries. We traversed through the town observing and learning the history and culture of the people in the area, many activities were going on and we enjoyed the on street piano performances and Pride matches which were taking place. After about an hour of walking and touring we came to the ending of the tour and it was time to board the ferry to also enjoy the beautiful water tour of the harbour and the far water way of the city. We all rushed in the ferry and many people were on board which included mostly elderly and few youths. As the ferry moves, we started to observe the many activities like fishing, transport and sporting which were taking place in Stralsund, I sat at the top section of the ferry to view and observe well the beauty of the place. Many people were taking picture and the captain of the ferry would give lessons about the harbour at each important point we reached at during the sail. The sail was so memorable as we saw many beautiful land feature and bridges which made the place beautiful. We also saw one of the historical ships which was said to have been used in the early 1800s during the wars of expansion and protection. It was so big and really looked old and ragged. The water trip was about one hour and we were back to the dock. After we claimed to go to the accommodation as some people were in need of refreshing and others wanted to take some rest. People who wanted to go by train to the accommodation were asked to follow the lady instructor and those who were strong enough to walk we followed the man instructor. We walked along the lake shores as the cold breeze penetrated our bones and the wind whirled in our ears. We passed via many sculpture of great men of the city and I also noticed that cycling was the best transport in Germany. After about 40min of walking while talking and making noise, we reached the place for residence for the next few days. Our luggage was already prepared and all we had to do was to get it and shuffle it to our rooms. We met Frank again at this point and we had a debrief of where to find our rooms and how to open them. Also we were told to refresh and meet again at some place where we were to have clubbecue. We followed some lady coordinator and went to the house with our rooms, we all got in and refreshed.

The clubbecue Night at Stralsund

It was about 8PM when everyone had already gone to the clubbecue place and being new in the area, I could not find my way to the meeting place. I asked for help in the common group which we had on media and I was directed to where the palace was. I hampered slowly to the place and never was I reaching till when I saw a group of people who were taking a smoke, I asked them whether they would direct me to the place where there were people having clubbecue. They directed me I think using the long way because I took long to get there. On reaching I met people already enjoying the feast and I was to just integrate in and start from where I found them. I got a piece roasted potatoes and a big bottle of soda before I waited for other things. I started right away once I sat down. There were many activities that were taking place and one of the professors was showing physique tricks of which some were really hard. He demonstrated the burning nature of hydrogen and also showed us the hydrogen powered automobiles.The night was moving well and people were happy and drunk, as you know ladies will always want the best and they were always in and out of the ride. After about two hours, I was feeling so tire and I could not continue any more but rather to take a nap, I decided to go back to my room but before I went some of the people we met there were from India and they had heard that someone on the program also came from India and hence they were eager to meet me which I never had in mind. As I set off to going back to my room, I was called in a very local India way Baya..., I knew that it was an Indian calling me. I turned my head and looked at them, as they approached me and they were so happy to meet me. They asked me whether I spoke Hindi when I told them I do not because I am not India but I just reside there for now three years of my education. They were very surprised and happy. I told them as I was soon leaving because I was so tired and they insisted that we should have a drink together at the moment as we talk. I told them as I was not an alcohol person and later I agreed to have a soda as they drunk their beer. They were as usual asking me many questions right from my name, country, which state I was studying in India, college and why I chose India of which some I could not answer and some questions were so personal that I would not share with anyone. After a while I left them and went to my room and had to talk with my family and get updates from my emails, having checked all that I went to sleep.

HOST day 1

Early morning, breakfast was to be taken, I grabbed my coupon and headed to the cafeteria for breakfast, and after a few hours we all gathered at Haus 4 where we were to start our day with a briefing and then headed for a tour of for the Lab at the Institute of renewable energy. We met a professor who took us through the process of making renewable fuels like Hydrogen and methane. The lab was one of the key manufacturers of hydrogen in Germany and we saw many sophisticated instruments which were used in the process. Hydrogen was extracted from this time from air and purified for commercial usage.He also showed us the different ways in which hydrogen was stored which included high pressure sealed tubes, chemical methods and liquification methods as well. We went further to observe the study about fuel cells which were used in hydrogen powered auto-mobiles, looking at each component one by one and illustrating how each is put together to make a complete fuel cell. The tour was closed by showing us a wind mill which by that time was laid down by strong wind from the sea, we looked at its parts and took pictures. Above all the lab tour was so magical that it made me see new technologies which were beyond my reach and I also learned more about why Hydrogen was the next sustainable green fuel for Humanity. We were adjourned for lunch, before that, Frank had asked us to book earlier for the train or bus to the airports of exit earlier yet I was not in position to do it by my own due to lack of credit card. I approached him and asked him to help. He took me to the HOST (Hochschule Stralsund) foreign students' officer who helped book the FLIX bus ticket for my departure which was scheduled for 2ndSeptember. She printed the tickets and gave them to me. I hurried to go to the mess hall of the University where our lunch was served. I met my friends and we took lunch together, after a few minutes Elisabeth told us we had about 20 minutes to the start of the next lecture and we had to hurry. We then moved to the lecture hall, and Prof. Kuhr was waiting, his lecture was the most informative of all and it was about" Turning the power of the sun into Hydrogen" As we entered the hall, it was highly computerised and funny enough he told us that he was given it to him for the first time so he had to be sorry for him once something goes wrong. Having entered, he started his lecture with a simple and reasonable question "What is hydrogen and why do we need it? and of course most of us we knowledgeable about hydrogen and some of its uses. Having asked that question and getting our opinions, he told us about what the sun was and what photons were and how much energy they carry. With a lot of physics and chemistry he explained how a photon of light can be used as energy to drive the process of splitting water molecules into hydrogen gas and oxygen. He explained the different ways in which the above process could be achieved and the feasibility of all the theoretical models. The professor concluded his lecture by showing us the different hydrogen powered machines like trains and power generation plants. The lecture was best in its kinds that it showed more insight about the sustainable fuel hydrogen was and the need for it to be our next hope for environmental pollution free energy. After a very exhaustive lecture we went to have some coffee and the next program on the list was visiting the brewery. I was so tired and called it off. I went back to my room and had some other things to do or even sleep or talk to family. When I reached my room, I switched on my phone and waiting for messages to sync. I then took a shower and got some coke from my fridge, poured in my glass with some ice cubes and switched on my laptop, I opened my emails because that is the first thing I treasure online. The reason is I apply for so many opportunities and also I mail many professors, coordinators and friends whom I expect to help in career and occupational search. After a while I opened my phone and viewed that I had missed a call, I was so socked because no one in Germany had my new number and no one had ever asked me for it. I decided to call back but the person never picked, I thought it was a scam call. I left it and continued, opened telegram and searched for some movies to keep the stress and tiredness out.

The Evening well spent

In a few minutes, I saw my phone lighting and it was the same number that called and I had not picked, I decided to pick and hear what they were telling me. I heard an young teenager's voice saying,Hello sir, I helped you buy a sim card, do you remember me? .I remembered that he had promised to call me but it was unbelievable as it had been almost two days.

Teenager: Sir, have you forgotten me? Me: No, please do not call me sir. call me Eidris. Teenager: Okay sir. My name is Alex Me: Okay Alex, How are you and why did you call? Alex: Eidris, I just called to say Hi, and maybe check on you and fulfil my promise because I told you I will call you and I had forgot till when I saw your picture on Instagram showing that you are in Stralsund. Me: Oh yeah, thank you very much. I arrived a few day back in Stralsund, and I was expecting your call days back. But its nice that you were truthful. Thank you man. Alex: Yeah, Eidris I am also in Stralsund, we came with my family to participate in national sports which was scheduled in Stralsund. Which part are you in maybe we can just meet and I tour you around. Me: Oh, I am in HOST (knieper Nord), and that will best for sure because I am little bored here in my accommodation. Alex: Wow, also our reservation is near Knieper Nord and lets meet at the bus station, hope you have your 9eticket. I will be there in five minutes Me: Okay Alex, lets meet in five.

In less than five minutes I was at the station and the next bus to that station was in 10 minutes, I was waiting. Alex came from the opposite direction from were I was looking and called me by name. I turned around and he was wearing like going for a summer beach party yet I was wearing like an Eskimos. Even though it was sunny, the temperature was lower than my used temperature in India, so I was feeling cold. When he reached we sat at the station and asked him where he was taking me for the evening. He stood up and went to the bus chart and said we are going to board the bus till the last point it stops then we go to the zoo and the largest shopping mall in the city of Stralsund then we will go to the beach at night my friends are having a party till morning. I was shocked by the plan which was in a young man's head. In a few minutes the bus arrived and we boarded, I asked him what kind of sports he does and he told me he was an athlete and he asked whether I do any sport, I told him I was not a sportsman and the games I try are indoor games. I liked his sense of humour and hospitality that he was making me feel not isolated in Germany at that moment because I was fearing to move alone and even had not talked with anyone about such issues of sports, and laughing with people. Even roaming around the city, and doing crazy things with no plans, and having to just be young again in my teenage age was the best thing he showed me that evening. Before I had wanted to behave like a principled, old person who is serious and strict but then I accepted to be in his age group and it helped me understand and enjoy the moment we spent together doing crazy staff. When I said I was more into indoor games and he whispered in my ear that "Which indoor bed games do you like most?, I had not integrated it well till when I saw him laughing then I got to know he was talking about stupid staff. I also told him all except Snaked and ladders . The bus was reaching stops and we were not getting out till when I asked him the stop we will get out from, he then said till when the driver says "I stop here".I was so socked and remember being a foreigner in a country we fear trouble and in Europe Police is more active than the other law suits. I accepted and he asked why I dont like snakes and ladders, I told him that because African snakes are very big and they cant climb ladders well so they end up falling with the ladders all the time. He had not gotten my humour and asked me whether its true there are very big snakes in Africa because he knew that most of them come from Amazon forests. I told him its a humour saying and then he understood what I was meaning and he laughed so loud that people in the bus looked at us. After some minutes the bus driver said he was at the last stop, then Alex went and asked him in German where we could find the zoo. He directed us and we had to walk around 5 minutes. I was wearing like Eskimos meaning I could not run yet Alex was wearing like these beach volley ball players and sports shoes, He then said lets run instead of walking, and before he finished he started and I was suffering with the heavy clothes and heavy shoes till when I walked when I was so tired. I found him at the Zoo gate already buying the tickets, when I arrived he was done and I was about to enter when they told me I was to be checked, and I had to leave my winter coat at the entrance. I was about to be harsh and Alex told me that it was fine we wont be there for long. We entered and there were many animals and birds, reptiles and insects. We wanted to go to the outside environment zoo but it was not allowed passed 8PM, so we stopped in the inside and went to watch some videos about wild life and went to VR (Virtual reality) simulations and it was very fun. Alex then started the issue of lifting each other as we went from one section to another, I agreed and we were going to the Birds section, around five stair cases up, I lifted him on my shoulders and he was quite heavy maybe 56kg to 60kg when we reached we saw many beautiful birds and some of which were rare and he started telling me history of birds that he knew and significance in their country.

As we moved through the section, I saw a crested crane which is my country bird and I was so happy and touched, I made noise which it makes and it turned around I was like crying. He asked me to tell him about it and why was it our country bird. I told him things i was told in school and then we had to move to the reptile section, it was his turn to lift me. He could not and I told him I will lift him in another style and like a baby, using my back. He was so exited but I was the most enjoying because I have never had a young brother to play with in this manner. We reached the reptiles and they were very many and scary. He told me many things about snakes and lizards. It was time we leave the zoo because time was rushing and buses were stopping to move by 10 PM, we rushed out chasing each other like playful brothers, I was really enjoying because it was some of the moments I have never gotten in my life. I had almost forgotten my winter coat, he remembered it and went back to pick it. We then had to go to the shopping mall, but I had no money and no plans to buying anything, I then asked him whether he was going to buy something and he said yes, and also to tour it because its so big. We waited for the bus at the station near the Zoo, in about 10minutes it came and we boarded. In the bus i told him, he created the some of the best memories in my life because I had never gotten such moments of being wild with someone or friends. He then put his head on my shoulder and asked me how old my next brother was, I told him 20years at the moment. He said just one year more than him but its almost then same. We then reached the stop to the mall, and we went out, crossed the road and went into the shopping mall. This was so big and beautiful with many stores and shops. I asked him what he was going to buy and he said nothing, he just wanted to come and move around all the different layers till the top. I looked at him and said you so fucked up, and he told me if he had said he was not going to buy anything, I would not have accepted to come

with him, and he was trying to apologise when I told him I knew
he was not going to buy anything because he looked down when
he was saying yes. The he asked me why I accepted, to come when
I knew the truth, I old him because I also wanted to see the
biggest mall and to also continue with the memorable wild
evening. We moved through all the layers of the mall, running and
entering different shops, trying different products and he was
taking picture and videos. We reached the perfume section he told
me what they used to do with his friends, that they could test all
the perfumes and go out of the shop smelling different types of
fumes and he suggested we did the same. I was into it because it
was not illegal, so we tested all the perfumes small samples only
but almost all. by the time we reached the last layer where an
elegant restaurant was, we were so tire and I was so mesmerised
about what I saw, the restaurant was so beautiful and organised
with digital menu cards, outside the windows one could see the
view of the city till the sea. He said we will take a cup of coffee
here and some snack then go. We sat and he ordered, I told him
that the items were expensive and he said that we were also
expensive. I kept shut and sat, they brought the coffee and snacks
I started eating, he was taking pictures and videos. Then after he
also joined, then he asked me whether I have ever been to dates, I
told him not many times but in my country and he told me to
consider this a brothers date. I laughed and told for sure, you seem
like a brother and maybe I will remember you as a brother from
Germany. He paid and we went to the buy and as we walked I
asked him, the next destination and he said we will go to the
beach and find his friends and have a night beach party with some
drinks and smoke. I told him as I never drink or smoke, and he
asked me whether I was muslim and I told him I was. He said, I
never looked like one but he will get me some sodas and then we
enjoy. I agreed and we boarded the bus, we reached Knieper Nord
around 20 minutes to 10PM when the sun was almost setting and

he told me to wait for him to bring the soda bottles then we slope to the beach. He came with four bottles and I asked him who will drink all that, and he said I was to drink them. I told him the maximum I can drink soda is two bottles, I noticed I was becoming the original me and I decided to say sorry. Then I go hold of two bottles and we sloped down. The party had already started and his friends asked him where he was when he told them about me and he introduced me. They asked him in German language when I saw him deny by his head, I never took it serious and I just tried to fit in. They were drinking, smoking and dancing. Girls and boys even though it was not my life but I was in for it this time, I tried old dance styles but it was not making sense for me. The I herd them speaking in German and pairing up, then one of them called me and said i can just choose anyone its just a dance, then I said the last person I will go with but they should first choose. The Alex was looking at me and I made for him a hand sign to mean what?, Is there any problem?. He nodded his head showing that no problem. The remaining girl came to me and held my hand and asked me whether I had ever tried dancing with someone before. I told her not and she told me she will teach me and I must follow the tune and her steps. We started and I was enjoying the dance, then we had to finish with a kiss, I did not want to do it because these were all random stranger, but the girl was telling me to do it or else its going to shame her, when I did so I heard other people clapping which I never expected. Then I asked her what they said in German, she just told me that she was the lucky and unlucky person in the group. I was shocked and decided to sit down as they continued to drink and smoke. The only thing I wanted at that time was going back and sleeping. Alex came and told me not to be angry about what the girl said, I asked him why did she say unlucky and he told me because most people don't fear kissing and it was common in Germany and she said she was lucky because she was the first in our group to kiss an

African. As he was speaking, he was moving his hands on my thighs and I pretended to not have noticed it. Then I asked him, why did he reject something they asked him and I was having a guess that it was about me. He said its not okay to talk about it at that time, I told him it was fine to say it. He asked me whether I will not get angry and send him off, I told him it was okay, he could say it however hard it was. He then said that they asked him whether I was him boyfriend. I asked him whether he was Gay or bisexual and he told me he was Gay. I was so socked and was about to explode but then I had promised not to destroy my evening. I cooled down and told him, it was fine no need to get scared. He then told me many stories about him being gay but my mind was not present at the moment. Because I was going to say that I was to dance with Alex as my new brother and all that started coming back. After a while he asked me whether I was okay and I told him I was fine. I told him, I wanted to go back as the next day I had alot on my schedule. He then agreed, and told me that he wanted to have some moments with me and tell me after but he never told me because I told him I was muslim. Then he decided to just keep it and take me as a friend and a little brother. I was socked but then realised that people who respect each others beliefs exist and they are good people regardless of their deeds. He took me back to the station near to my accommodation. Before I left him, he apologised and I told him he had no problem and he was the most open minded person I had ever met because he knew my religion and respected, and there fore I respected him. I told him he was still my friend and I like him as my little brother, I hugged him and told him that we will meet again some other day.

The Free Day

Later the next day after the beach party, I woke up very tired. Having taken shower, I was looking for what to eat because I had missed dinner last night and checking on the time, it was past breakfast time. I took a bus and went to the market place where I opted to find where to get anything to eat. Most of my colleagues whom we were on the program had boarded for other states in Germany since it was a free day and we had no program from morning till the next day. On checking my phone I had a lot of messages from friends, family and even some of the colleagues were calling me for hiking but I was still asleep and they had gone already. After taking some cold coffee, I went down the beach to observe how beach life in the summer is in Germany. Reaching, everyone was on their own swimming, sunbathing and others playing. I got a sunny spot and sat in the sand, I decided to call my aunt on video but due to time difference she was asleep and most people I was to interact with were far and not online by then. I decided to enjoy the nature, beautiful sea songs, wind and people socialising and interacting. After a few minutes, a group of men in their early 20s around 23 to 25 years came by and they were going to play beach soccer. The were seven people and amongst them was a black. They came laid their stuff in sand and tuned the music on, pulled out drinks and removed their shirts on. They were just a small distance away from me and I was silently watching them. I wanted to join them because I was bored and they were in my age group. After some few minutes I saw the black guy approaching towards my space and called me "Hi, do you want to join us in soccer. We are seven yet we need to be equal to make two small teams." I agreed and went to where they were. The black guy told me he was Dan (Daniel), from South Africa and the other six were his course mate and two were from Germany while the remaining four were from different countries but in Europe and they all were studying in a Berlin but had come to Stralsund for summer holiday. I was happy to socialise with people again and again because everyday was a new day for adventure and I was really enjoying.I am not a sportsman and I don't play soccer but I had to try just to fit in group. We started and made two balanced teams as me and Dan were in opposite teams. Because I was feeling a little cold due to weather, I told them that one team should have shirt on and the other off. Now the challenge was I had only underwear and trouser on, with no shorts. I told them I would play in trousers if they dont mind and one of them said, " No, you just need to remove and stay with what ever you have inside or nothing." I was socked and Dan told me it was fine we were all men and moreover most people do sunbathing, swimming when they are naked on beaches in Germany so it was no big deal. I was so worried and I hovered my eyes to look at people who were swimming till when my eyes landed on two men who were fully naked and one lady who was naked sunbathing of which I had not been seeing them due to my absent mindedness that something like that could not be possible.

Enjoying with the strangers

So putting aside the nude beach issues, we had to start the soccer. I removed the trouser and stayed in my underwear and my shirt. The game started and we were playing it well. I enjoyed with these guys till when we looked around and almost everyone was looking at us and some teenagers came and wanted to join. We had no option and we dived them into the two teams and we continued to play. I was just playing to enjoy, and when it was about 4PM, we finished the game. I was to go back to HOST accommodation when Dan came and asked me whether I would like to go with them to their hotel, they had eats and drinks and they also had plans to go to the city spa for massage. I told them I was having some other programs and I had to prepare today for them. Dan told me they will be paying everything and since I had the 9eticket transport was not an issue. I was just waiting for them to say that and when Dan told me, I told them it was fine but I was not to go with them in the spa for massage. We went to the bus station and in about 5 minutes, the bus arrived and on boarding, we waited for a few stops and we had reached the hotel. They had rented an apartment on the forth floor for all of the seven and had different bedrooms which some where tin sharing and two were master bedrooms as Dan told me. I sat down by the sitting room with a very big wide screen and I was pretending to watch it, yet I was in fear that maybe these guys were not what they told me and I was so frightened because the place was looking so elegant and expensive. After few minutes, Dan came and told me to go take a shower as they had ordered for eats in a few minutes they were to reach. I denied and he asked me the reason why and I told him I don't use people's towels for bathing and neither do I use shower in places I dont know. He laughed and told me to get serious as I was playing with them and sweated, I felt offended but then I realised it was my mistake that I tried to bring silly principles. I agreed and went into the shower. I entered the shower and I cant narrate the technology I saw, music system was embedded in the wall, temperature knobs were digital and towel dispenser was digital in which used towels were dropped somewhere and each time one had to take a shower a fresh towel is given by their desire. It was really next level to me. I finished showering and when I went out I was not seeing my clothes, Dan told me he had collected it and placed it into the washer and in about one hour, I would get it when they were clean and dry because he used a quick wash program and in a mean while I was wearing the shower hood. All the seven people were sitting in the sitting room and most of them were on their phones, I sat down by the empty

seat and Dan called me to sit next to him. When I sat, they all
started to ask me questions one after the other, from where I was
from, original country, why I had come to Germany, and why I
was studying in India. there were many question and I am sure I
answered a few. One of them went and brought two bottles of
wine, and glasses. Basing on the looks of the bottles, the wine
must have been expensive and I told Dan that I dont drink or
smoke. He then stood up and got a bottle of soda. One of the
friends asked me why I was not drinking yet I was a young man. I
told them it was because of my beliefs and health issues. In a few
minutes, the bell went and one of them went to check when, the
had ordered a huge meal and as they started to unpack it I asked
them whether they had ordered some vegetarian dish, and Dan
told me that one of their friend was vegetarian and one dish was
for him. Before he finished the fellow who was vegetarian
accepted to share with me and all was set, then Dan asked me how
it was possible to be an African and vegetarian and I told him and
I could not explain. We ate as they were all on their phones and in
about an hour I asked Dan to get me my clothes and he did. The
vegetarian guy always looked at me in a shy way and when I was
going to wear I went to the wall side and I saw him by the
reflection looking at me. After a while, one of them stood up and
said that it was time to go to the spa they had seen nearby for
some massage. I was not to join because I had never been in
anything like that and even I was fearing. They all stood up and
started to move outside, me and Dan went out last and we waited
for the elevator, on reaching down one of them asked Dan
whether I agreed to go with them and Dan answered yes. I was
frightened more, we then went to the bus station and I asked them
as they said the massage spa was near and then why were we
using the bus. One of them answered that it was just three bus
stops from the hotel. the bus arrived then, and we boarded.
Everyone was on their phone and I was looking outside observing

the city. It was around 7PM and the sun was almost setting. After about three bus stops, we went out and climbed a few stair cases to a beautiful reception and one of them spoke in German, we were led to the first flow where we were to get the massage from. It was my first time and I think last but it was more fun, relaxing and inciting at the same time.

The Massage and Steam-bath

We were put into duo-sharing rooms and unlucky I was put with the vegetarian who was looking at me always. The two ladies to work on us told us to enter into the changing room and rap the towel from the umbilicus to down, the towel was rectangular long in length but not in width that it covered till the knees. I was feeling ashamed and fearing to get out. I then swallowed a pin, and I went outside of the dressing room and already the other guy was being massaged, the lady told me to lay facing down and straighten my hands forward and legs backwards. I wont estimate the age of the lady or girl who was working on me but based on her hands and the softness of her touch, she seemed to be virgin and not exceeding 25 years. I will be frank and I will say what really happened to my body. The place was having this ambient atmosphere, scents of roses and mint were everywhere, the slow relaxing music made the whole process 100% perfection. The first thing I felt on my back was drops of soft oil which were spread to my whole back by soft soothing hands, I started groaning in melody and sweetness, I was feeling vibrations through my whole body because it was the first time I had a total submission of my body to anyone. My weakest spot is the armpits and nipples, so I was scared to feel ones hands on them and I was ready to make loud noise and laughters. The lady or girl but lady seem old school, we will use girl. The girl massaged my back and every point in my back joints felt the process, as she went down I was very scared that she will untie my towel and massage the African butt, but I was so lucky that the service was for back, hands, legs and chest followed by steam bath them facial. As she went to my legs, I was so deepened in the process that I never wanted it to stop, as professional as she did everything, I was so enjoying and after that it was time for the turn over and during the process protocol is that the client has to be turned and lay on their spine. I never agreed and I turned myself, as I saw my other friend he was in the best moods, and his penile region had grown a hump. I told the girl to be slow and not to touch anywhere near by penile regions, else if she seems me saying no in some places, she should not continue. The girl agreed and she started by the thorax region and was massaging my chest a lot with more emphasis on my nipples, then I started to laugh and told her to stop, she went to the belly region of which I had no problem because it has no ABS that it will be attractive but rather to cause opening of the sphincter is she presses it hard. In about an hour the first session was done and we had to meet with out friends in the steam bath room. I went on laughing and covering my nipples with my fingers, reaching the steam place, it was a little hot and Dan called me to sit next to him, he started asking me whether I liked it and how often do I go for it, I told him it was nice and relaxing though it was my first time. We talked more with Dan and he was telling me more about his family and his studies, during the process I was sweating so much and Dan told me, that if I wanted I can go to the next room where the was a jacuzzi for the time which was remaining, I decided to go there of which I had never been in one before. While I went, the vegetarian guy followed me also and I did not know, I met no one in the jacuzzi and I was entering with my towel, when he told me not to enter with towel. He removed his towel without any shyness and threw it away and entered. I was shocked and feared to enter, as I was standing he said there were only 20 minutes remaining to the end of the session we had paid. I knew I could not get the chance again and I also removed and covered my genitals with my hands as I entered in. Warm scented water, I was feeling so fine because those were the things I only saw in movies. The guy was moving towards me and I was fearing him already ever since he started looking at me when ever I am naked, he started asking me questions and I was answering him, and he wanted to touch me by the shoulder when I moved away, as he was trying to talk about himself, Dan came and told me if I wanted to go for facial treatment. I agreed and I went off the jacuzzi and the guy was still looking at my butt, as I moved out. We went to the facial and I told them that it was my first time and if it wasn't good for my face I can forego it. They said it was fine and I got my first facial treatment, after about 30 minutes, it was done and we were given some drinks of which I never knew which drinks were I asked for a glass of water instead. We finally had come to an end, on looking at the time, it was almost 10PM and I told them I had to go back to my accommodation to organise my things for tomorrow's program. The told me they were heading to some club for the rest of the night and I left them boarding a bus when I stood by the road to find out how to reach Knieper nord. I went to the nearby station and the next bus was the last one and was in about one hour. The day was well spent and full of nice events and things I never thought I would do in my life.

Berlin Again

The next day we had to go to the Hiddensee Island as part of the Sustain MV program. Due to the exhaustive day I had, the day before with the strangers, I woke up very late and the team day already reached the harbour to catch the ferry to the Island. I tried to hurry and take shower, breakfast, ran to the bus station. Reaching the station I was told that buses never worked that day due some activities which were going on (the sports which Alex had told me about). I asked people the easiest way to the harbour and they were all not well with English. I had to walk to the harbour which was about 20 minutes walk and the ferry was leaving in 30 minutes. I was at the junction and never knew which road to take. I met a woman who directed me and as I was moving I saw one of my team mates also coming towards my side and I decided to wait for her. When she reached I asked her where she was heading and she told me to the harbour and I told her we had to hurry because the ferry was leaving in 30 minutes. She then told me that I was suing a very long way and her google maps were showing her another short direction. I agreed and we decided to run to the harbour before the ferry took off. We ran, the lady was from Vietnam and before we even reached the middle of the journey, they texted a message in the group that the ferry had departed. She then asked me what we should do, and I had no idea, I told her we could go back and do other things in our accommodations, and she asked me that things like what? I had no answer, she then said, she has slept enough and could not go back and get bored, I then told her since we had our 9eticket, we could go to the train station and go to either Berlin or Frankfurt or any other state in Germany and visit it. She agreed and she decided Berlin because she had never been there, as she came through Frankfurt airport. I told her, we had to move very fast because the trains were scars and the journey was very far about 3 to 4 hours.

We then checked using her phone for the nearest train station and it was Stralsund Hauptbahnhof. The train was in 30 minutes and it was a little far, we decided to walk and run at the same time.We were able to make it on time and entered the train. We had a long journey of about 3 hours and reached Berlin Hauptbahnhof. As described earlier, it was the same and this time it was a little more cold. We went out of the train and moved to the first level, went out of the station, basing on how she was wearing, it was really cold for her as she was not a native of the place but wearing like natives in summer. We went to the nearest street beneath the bride, and we ordered some burgers, plus sodas. she had at first refused to eat but then I persuaded her to and we ordered together.

As we finished to take the burger, she decided to go and visit other places in Berlin I never knew and I also decided to visit the museum and other places in Berlin. We went together to the park and that is where we separated.I decided to move using maps looking for the museum, once I checked and the museum had closed that day, I decided to roam around, I visited the beautiful buildings and parks in Berlin. I once met celebrity photo shoot near a big cream white building which gave a very beautiful view. I went further down the road and met a movie scene being shot, I stood there for about 30 minutes, and it was a spectacular moment when I saw the actions being done. At that same spot, I saw a man who was looking at me, and when he saw I was seeing he, then he approached me. He introduced himself to me and told me to be curious because there were many pickpockets in Berlin. I was wearing my stretchy Yoga pants with zipped pockets. I was then keen and curious, after a while I sloped down when I saw people were sitting by the river, I went and sat too and took come picture due to the beautiful view and the place was so calm and cool plus the mild sun which was shinning. After a while I went to the bus station and observed where I could go, I was asking myself where to go when I heard someone saying they were going to the visit the concentration camp (Sachsenhausen), I wanted to join them by taking the bus they were to take when I received a call from my Vietnam friend I came with that she was heading back because the place was so cold for her and she could not handle the coldness. I ran back to the station looking for her, on reaching she had boarded the train and the next was in about 2 hours. I went and sat in the Moabit Prison Historical Park which was once an once a place of "cries" and execution now stands a beautiful part for resting, picnic and strolling. It was a bad trip because I never got a chance to visit the places I wanted because they were all closed, the Futurium the Germany's known museum of futuristic technologies with biggest 3D printers, robots and artificial intelligence technologies. What pained me most was the desire I had to visit the Berlin Museum of Medical History which is said to house the history of medicine over the last 300 years, extensive collections focusing on pathology and human anatomy, former operating theatre, a pathologist's dissection room, a laboratory and a patients ward. As I was sitting in the park wasting some time till the next train could arrive while I was reading about the places I was to visit a girl approached me with her dog and sat next to me. She asked me some few question and told me whether I was interested in Berlin city tour, she was a volunteer in the city tour program which was cheaper and lasted only 3 hours. I was forced to ask her how much it was and secondly I asked how she knew that I was new in Berlin because she would have gone to other people in the park. She told me, I was the only one wearing yoga pants in the part, which were not common in Berlin, and that I was the only one wearing winter sweater in summer in Berlin which was common to foreigners. I was surprised and I told her I was having a train to catch in about an hour, she was a very beautiful girl and was making me shy as I talked with her because she was looking direct in my eyes. So I told her not to stare at me so much, she then said we should go at Restaurant ParisMoskau as she said most tourists who visit Berlin atleast visit that restaurant. I agreed, and we walked a few meters and reached, I was nervous and shy to this girl because she look so cute, young and straight forward that she was not fearing to talk to strangers which is not common in Africa and India. She asked me a lot of questions as usual where I was from, why I was visiting Germany and Berlin specifically, till when she went too far and asked about my relationships when I refused to tell her she started to trick me and I told her that she was making me nervous because most girls in Africa and India where I lived rarely talk to men or boys like that. Then she tried to show that she was just trying to interact with me and that was all. We spent about more 20 minutes and we were talking till when they brought the bill and I waited to see whether she will the that the bill was on her, she didn't, I was shocked yet the bill was almost finishing my whole money I had in my pocket. I paid and she told me that I was waiting for her to say that the bill was on her. Then I wondered how she knew it, I then had to leave her and before I left, she asked me when I was going back to India because I had told her that I will be back to Berlin to board for India. When I told her she gave me her Instagram user ID and told me to message her once I reach and she then said I was a good man, rare to find and calm. I was really in sock and nervous because I was having less than 20ein my pockets and the girl was like a spy knowing even my next steps, not shy at all and straight forward. This was on he things I had taken long to see.

I then went back to train station, and the train was about 5 minutes to reach. I waited and I boarded and it was around 7PM when we started the journey of 3 hours. I got to charge my phone in the train, when I saw I had missed a call from Alex, I never called him back and checking my instagram, he had sent me a message and pictures telling me that he had become second in the marathon which was that day and had secured his study grant. I texted him back that I was happy for him. Immediately he saw the message he called me, and we talked, he asked me whether I watched the sports which was that day and I told him I was from Berlin at that time and he was asking me many questions of which I told him it was part of the program that brought me. He was okay with it and asked me the time I was to reach, I told him that I would be late and since I was tired, I was to just go to and have shower and take a nap. He agreed and asked me when I was to leave Stralsund which I told him on 2 nd yet that day was 28th and he asked me whether we could meet again at he beach the next day at around 9PM as they were organising a party before they were to leave Stralsund. I was about to deny when he told me that Ann (the girl that I danced with last time and we kissed)was asking if she could meet me again for dance, I was then intrigued to go back. I agreed and ended the call. After reaching my destination, I rushed to get the last bus to Knieper nord, it was just a few minutes and I was on time. In a few minutes, I was at my accommodation, took a shower and went to sleep.

CHAPTER SEVEN

Sustain MV 3

We were soon reaching the climax of the program "Sutain MV, 2022" and we all were enjoying the exiting moments. The program was all moving smoothly and perfectly. We were going to visit again another amazing place Neubradenburg. Waking up in the early morning as usual, shower and race for breakfast. Our bus was waiting at Haus 4, ready to drive a 2 hour journey to a new town of Neubradenburg, we all hurriedly moved very fast to reach the bus station. The bus had to take us to the train station, we reached a few minutes to the departure of the train and entered quickly. During the journey we passed through different beautiful places having green fields with many wind plants. It was actually like Greifswald. I was seated just at the window observing all the nature. I was taking pictures of the different places we passed through and making them into photo-grids. I also never forgot my back-pack which always contained my utilities like charger, and I had my friend's power bank. The drive was very long and many people were sleeping when I saw one of the ladies seated in the next section from me, and she moved closer to the empty seat next to me and we had a cool jazz. She was from Brazil and most times when we hear the word Brazilian ladies, we all know what comes in our minds. She was so beautiful and calm, her eyes were amber grey and had wore a rose scented perfume, with no make-up and her lips were just masked with lip-bum, as she talked, I looked at the alignment of her teeth and white in color. She was good in IT and photography, and I asked to see some of her work samples when she showed me her pictures she takes during every moment in Sustain MV, I was stunned and amused. She also promised to be taking me some pictures. I further asked her whether she loved to stay in Brazil or she would wish to stay in other places. She then asked me whether I was proposing to her and I was shyly ashamed. she then told me that most men propose in that way. She then told me that she was more into creating a positive change in her country more so the community where she lives. She told me about her project she was currently working on about developing an application that could allow all students to have access to free open source materials and software for academic development.

Neubradenburg Day

We reached Neubradenburg a little late at around 12 noon and could not make the city tour. At the station we crossed the busy road and sloped down, reaching the main city gate and we crossed through. There were beautiful houses, churches and theatres. Along the walk ways were red marked signs which indicated bike ways, it was my first time to see such, this was highly followed by the people. We walked for about 10 minutes and finally we had reached the beautiful university HOST-Neubradenburg. We were welcomed and they gave us gift bags which contained book, pen, stress ball and key holder. In no time, we were told to head for lunch as we delayed in the train and reached late when it was almost lunch time. We headed to the cafeteria, before we could start making food selections as most people were deciphering the prices and the types of foods served, the Foreign Student's Director told us that the lunch was pre-paid by the HOSTNeubradenburg Institution. This was like a love melody, I was trying to picture how much I was going to eat for that day because I was not even making upto 5 ein my pocket. On hearing the statement that lunch was pre-paid, I grabbed two plates, and one was for fruits and vegetables while the other was for food and on the same carry plate, I placed two bottles of soft-drink. My fruits and vegetables plate contained almost all the fruits served, and most vegetables I saw on the serving menu. My food plate contained rice because I had not tasted it ever since I arrived in Germany, and I was Hony for it, followed with potatoes and eggs, I was so much in love with the food. I brought it on table and everyone was looking at me as if they were saying I will waste it. But one thing I discovered in Germany was wastage of food and fruits is not a thing they do. Anyway I was not minding about who was looking at me or not but I was happy that I finally could eat the way I feel I had to eat. Where I sat, one of the friends asked me whether I will finish the food or not, I just told him to watch and see if even a single grain of rice remains, I will pick it and eat it also. He was shocked and just had to look at me. In about half an hour, I was done with the second soft-drink, and my policy is I only drink when food is finished. I was seated not facing everyone and when I finished, I was just waiting to see the first person stand up and then I could also stand and take my plate because its not in me to stand first on the lunch table. Suddenly I had a voice in my back asking me whether I still needed anything. I was surprised and I looked back to see was the coordinator Frank when I told him I could use a couple of cake slices. Everyone was socked and they all said What!!! I then smiled and Elisabeth then said as we had only five minutes to got to the first lecture, there was no chance for the cake slices and I headed to put my plates.

One of my of the people we came with came and asked me whether I was not feeling uncomfortable when I asked why? He then told me that I had eaten much food. I calmly told him I was feeling happy and okay, more so that food was normal to me and I could eat about the same as I ate to get to much food status. He just laughed thinking I was joking yet I was speaking the truth. We took the plates on the washing section and headed to the lecture hall.

The afternoon lecture went wild.

The lecture was about "Resilience to Climate Change & Sustainability in Urban Planning" given to us by Professor Mertens. As most lectures, we were meant to listen to the professor and take notes then after we ask questions where we had doubts. In her lecture, we started with questions, she was a very welcoming and smart lady who always wanted to learn and understand the perspective of her students. Unlucky, I am not an environmental student so the people who had more interest were the ones in love with nature and protection. Her lecture was more focused on the way modern technology has been used to shield the cities and towns from catastrophes. She showed us her research she made in USA following the major flooding in different cities, effects of cyclones, Katrina and other strong storms on the cities and the people. She further explained how urban planning has helped the world build resilient and sustainable structures which can with stand these environmental challenges. Her lecture was a long one because it was from 1 PM to 4 PM and we had to have a break of about 30 minutes. The first 2 hours were very fruitful and we enjoyed the lecture but how did the lecture get wild. When we finished the 2 hours we had to take a break and we had two option but also could do both, one was to get a cup of coffee and the other was to get up stairs and visit the bee houses as well as have an eagle eye view of the campus. After a about half an hour, we were back in the lecture hall. She continued with her discussion but this time she gave the floor to us and many people were having the knowledge about the urban planning and other related stuff. I was not feeling involved in the discussion. I started feeling sleepy and tried all I could to make myself a wake but it was not allowing. I tried moving out and back but it was all in vain. The discussion was so hot and beautiful but my situation was not normal. Then I remembered I had taken a lot of food and much sugary beverages. I tried to move down the coffee vending machine and grabbed on cup. I took some and then in less than thirty minutes, I was feeling alert and okay. The lecture was so nice but I never got to know about the ending because I was in the wash-room for about one hour. I had ate too much food but besides that, I had consumed more vegetables of which some were immersed in some organic oils and sprinkled some cheese yet my intestinal make up is not friendly with cheese. By the time I came out of the wash-room, I was one of the hungriest people around. It was at that time when I heard Elisabeth say that we were to have a clubbecue before we leave, I was like a saved man from drowning. We headed to the clubbecue grill and sat by the tables organised, drinks were plenty and edibles like vegetables, chicken, ham and cheese. I hurriedly grabbed a 1.5 litre Mango juice pack and opened it, with my mouth I was drinking, when one of the people asked me why I was using my mouth. I told her, I was marking my juice such that I would be the only one to drink it. She was wondering which kind of selfish person I was but that was not the meaning of what I was telling. We ate, drunk and enjoyed the moment in Neubradenburg amidst the enjoyment, there was a very beautiful, calm and open minded Brazilian lady who was offering her masters of science in environmental biology, her name was Juliana and it was her birthday. We heard the loud voice from her friends singing the birthday son with a tasty cake, and she was really happy as she never expected it and we enjoyed her new age with a beautiful celebration. The other challenge was I love cakes, and I was so turned on, when she reached my table I kindly requested her to leave the whole plate and go for another one to serve others. She left the plate and I enjoyed the full plate of cake, with my mango juice. after some time Setara and I went in the field to play together with others, we played for about half an hour and then we had to leave to catch the last train back to Stralsund.

The stranger on the train.

We moved to the train station and reached when the train was about to depart for Stralsund, hardly we could get it if we delayed a few minutes. We then entered and the section all my mates sat in was full and I had to go to the next section, there was only on duo-space and one chair was occupied by a gorgeous lady whom I never thought I would start a conversation with but luckily once I sat down, she looked at me, and I was having the black eye-shades on. I removed them and wanted to look back when she shyly looked away. I was also ashamed to look at someone who was not looking at me. After about 30 minutes of her pretending to be on phone, I asked her whether she knew the time the train will reach Stralsund. She then checked her phone using the DB-navigator application, she told me. But I knew the time only that I wanted to find a way of starting a conversation. Having told me the time, she then kept quite and I noticed that I never started the conversation well, so I had to look for another way. I then looked outside when it was about to start setting, I then said that all beautiful sunsets are signs to beautiful nights. She was hearing me and then she laughed and asked me whether I was a literature student. I told her I wasn't but I was fascinated with literature and writings of famous poets like Wole Soyinka, William Shakespeare and others. She then she was a major in literature and she was good in poetry. I told her whether I could get a chance to read some of her poems, and she never accepted but then she showed me her blog-website which she was trying to develop and aimed at unveiling the literature and poetry of Stralsund. I was really starting to enjoy her, and then she asked me what my majors were,if at all I was still in studies. I told her I was majoring in Biotechnology and she was surprised. she then asked me whether I can make the next COVID-19, and she then told me I looked more of a lousy guy. I told her not all books are the same even though they might be talking on the same topic.

She then argued that I said the metaphor wrong and she corrected me that it should be not to judge a book by its cover. Then I told her, I don't my saying was correct but she had never heard it before. She then asked me how old I was and why was I in Germany because I never looked to be a citizen nor a residence of any nature. I told her I was a student and she rejected that I was not a student in Germany, I asked why she was saying that and the obvious answer was, I asked her the arrival time of the train to Stralsund, then I asked her why would that meant that I am not a student in Germany. She then told me that all students in Germany use public transport and DB-navigator is a must-App on their phone and why was I not having it. She also told me the second reason was I was looking at her and not using my phone from the time I entered the train because I never had connection and when I reached the train I removed my sun-shades. I was really astonished by her character and observational skills. I then told her she was 90% correct. She then asked me the wrong observations she made, I told her I was having network connection on my phone and then I showed it to her, and she asked me why I never used my phone when I entered yet almost everyone will do that. I told her that I wanted to see the sun set and also to talk with her. She then laughed, but later became silent. I told her she was a very good observer and I also told her what I observed about her once I entered. I told her I saw her looking at me once I approached her sitting section, and then she shyly pretended not to be looking at me, she tried to reject but then I asked her how she saw me remove the eye-shades, because I was not yet seated when I removed them. She then agreed that she was looking at me but she never wanted to talk to people in public transport and even worse to strangers. I asked her whether I was making her uncomfortable when she said no. I told her my age and she told me I looked to be younger, I then asked her whether she was living in Stralsund or she just came to visit. She told me she was visiting her friends for about a week. I then asked her what her name was but she then told me I will know once we talk on instagram. We then had much conversation about Germany as she told me about the history and she told me about her life and why she chose to study history and literature. I also told me that I was from India and she asked me how I could be from India when I was an African, and I asked her why was she saying so and I told her that citizenship is not based on color and looks its ones right. But then I told her the truth that I was from an African country of origin but India was where I take my studies. She then asked where I was accommodating in Stralsund and I told her, and she told me that it was not far from her friends home where she was heading. Before I started another conversation, she asked me to send her a message on Instagram once I am free to visit her and her friends. I accepted and she gave me her handle on Instagram. She then asked me why I was in Germany and I had to explain to her the whole thing where it started and how it was going. After complete three hours, we reached the station we were to abort the train, as I said goodbye to her, she promised to text me on instagram so that I can visit her and her friends. I had to go and find my team because i would get lost and yet she was also getting off at the same station but going her own ways. We then rushed to the bus station to get the last bus to Knieper Nord. Luckily we arrived a few minutes before the bus could arrive and we safely boarded and in a few minutes we were at our place of accommodation. I reached freezing and I had to warm up with a cup of coffee, I processed it in my place and entered the bed, immediately I went to instagram and I sent the lady on the train a message. She never replied and I was little disappointed, and as any other person I started to think alot and even getting stressed out, thinking whether I made some mistakes or wrong things during our talks and that was why she was ignoring my messages. I was so worried, not because I was going to lose that first time relationship of friendship but because it was my first time to have a nonacademic conversation for such a long time. I had to relax myself and put my self to neutral point and consider it as a new step to life. With in no time I felt asleep and waited for the day tomorrow.

Wismar Day

In the morning of the following day, my hands immediately looked for my phone and having seen it I checked my Instagram to see whether my train lady replied, she had done so and even tried to call me on audio chat but I was in dream land by that time. I replied to her and maybe she was still asleep and tired because she left me a message saying they had gone to the beach for partying and drinking. I hurried to wake up, refresh, and catch the breakfast before the trip to Wismar could be no more for me. Having reached the breakfast point, I saw my colleagues were leaving for the bus when I asked them whether the time was then or I could get breakfast and meet them. Suddenly I heard Elisabeth's voice telling me to hurry and she said we had only 20 minutes to the departure of the bus to Wismar. I hurried and in a few minutes I was done with breakfast, then packed two apples in my back-pack just in case I got hungry before lunch. It was a 2 hour journey to Wismar, and we were joined by the Director of Foreign student's affairs at University of Wismar. We first visited the section of Applied sciences where we met many professors who took us in a tour about the different research projects which were being held at the section. From Biochemistry, applied chemistry, Biotechnology and environmental research, all these were the different Mega-sections with major research funded buy the different governmental and non-government organisations. We also had a lecture from Professor Stollberg of the section of mechanical and environmental sciences. Demonstrations of science experiments were done. Also we had beautiful but tiresome city tour of Wismar, where we saw many beautiful places and learned about the history of Wismar. The harbours, boats and ships were the main feature of the place, leaving that a side we had a good mean at the end of the program and it was so calming and refreshing. As the day was about to end I remembered that I had sent messages to someone in the morning and I to check them out and I was having many beautiful replies which made my day much more colourful. We ended by heading back and exhausted team of Sustain MV, we all were looking for sleep and relaxation except me and some few who had programs.

The chocolate Challenge.

During the lecture the professor told us about how the brain is able to create a difference in things regardless their indifference but because someone was told that certain things are different. He presented to us two cans where each contained a piece of square cut chocolate rapped in fol paper with labelled X and Y, and during his words he said that they were trying to carry out an experiment to show the difference between the quality of chocolate based on the fineness of the sugar used. He told us that basing on the quality and fineness of the sugar used in making chocolate, the price and longevity of the product. We all agreed because it was true and thus he told us that each of us was to be given only one piece of chocolate from each can and then we will follow what he would say. It was at that time when I asked him whether we were going to eat the chocolate pieces or not, he then told all of us that we were to eat the pieces as part of the experiment. We all were waiting for his instructions. The professor went further and explained how our tasting mechanism works and briefly elaborated basing on the anatomy of the tongue and the control of the brain during tasting. After a few minutes, he laid down three simple rules for the experiment.

• Carefully peal off the foil and observe the taste item first. • Bite slowly the chocolate and allow it move onto your tongue masticating slow and gently. • Swallow and carefully spot the sweetness. • Lastly rinse your mouth with water and repeat the same for the X or Y piece depending on your preference.

We all did as instructed and ate the two chocolate clubs. We were about 47 people and we all had a big challenge to either spot the difference or acknowledge that the two were the same. The professor then drew a table to quantify the number of people who had spotted the difference in the two chocolate clubs and those who did not. Among the 47 people almost three quarters spotted the difference including me and few people never did. After a few minutes when we all discussed the difference in taste, the professor said, that the two chocolate were the same but because he had initially implanted the thought of them being different, our brain looked for ways in which it could make the initial given information to be true. We were all surprised and could not believe we spotted the differences which were not even existing. After that mind blowing experiment we headed for lunch and other agenda.

The City tour, Harbour cruise, and dinner.

When lunch was done, we were led to the city tour by the local tour guide who was arranged for our team. She made us tour the different corners of the city, markets and churches which were beautiful places filled with sceneries and best for creating moments. Many people were so happy visiting these places, we further went to the harbour where we saw many beautiful activities like fishing, boat riding and ferries. A few big boats were at the harbour and they told us that they were for heavy voyages hence they do not move often, at the further point we were showed the boat making house. After about one and half hours, we headed to the ferry pickup point. We boarded for the harbour cruise tour which was estimated to take about one more hour. During the cruise we clearly observed the harbour and looked at the far ends of the city of Wismar. After the cruise we headed to the place where dinner was organised. The lady who was leading us thorough the whole day gave us a farewell talk at the dinner place, she was a very nice and sweet lady by her words and even basing on the hospitality we got, it was all more than what we could imagine. After her talk she told us that the University had paid for us the dinner but the drinks were on our budget. So we started ordering drinks, as we wait for our dinner. The hotel place was a very nice one and executive, we were served the drinks and a few minutes later the waiter told us that our buffet was ready and we had to do a self service at a section just below the executive lounge we were in. The buffet was mixed vegetarian and non-vegetarian, and enough for as many rounds as one could go. After eating, I went out of the dinning place and checked my messages on instagram, I found many messages of the lady I met at the train. By the way her name was Dennie, she had sent a message that if I would be free at around 9 PM I would message her. I then asked my team mate when the bus was to be leaving for Stralsund, and he told me we were about to be leaving. It was almost 6 PM, I then calculated the time we would be at the accommodation site once the journey starts. I then replied to her message that I was not going to be busy, thus she can tell me her plans for the night. At that time she was not online and I never got a reply, I had to wait. After about 20 minutes, we were called to the bus and we boarded, we then started our journey back to Stralsund. Once I entered the bus I checked my messages and I was having a message from Dennie, she told me whether I could meet them at the beach side by 9 PM with her friends as they have a night picnic and they had organised some eats and drinks and they were planing to be there till morning (Sunrise). I accepted and told her I was in bus coming back once I reach I will notify her and then I would slope by the beach as well. It was a two and a half hour journey and I got time to rest in the bus thus once I reached the accommodation I was able to refresh and headed to the beach side.

The night till sunrise.

I reached and sent to her a message, when she replied that I should look for the group of people who were having a big music speaker with lights on. The beach was having a lot of people arranged in groups with each group having its own motive and entertainment. I moved a bout 20 meters, where I saw the group she described and I told her I was standing near in a white winter jacker with the hood on. I saw her looking for me, when I called her and she came running and told me she thought I would not come. She then pulled me and told me she was to introduce me to her friends. Her group was about seven people with four females and two males, they were all happy and one of the ladies said that she thought I was a giant, and I felt offended but I had to keep it low. One of the males whom I knew by the name Allan, called me to sit by his side and he grabbed me a drink, I told him I was non-alcoholic, he then gave me a Fanta soda which was the only one left. What I discovered was that they could mix the soda and alcohol then drink, so I was supposed to be cautious. Dennie then asked me whether I wanted something to eat when I said I would be grateful, she then asked me what I would like because they had sausages, ham and steak. I told her that I was vegetarian then she just gave me salads and some bread. They started asking me some questions and I was happy to answer them. What I got to know was among the seven people there were two couples and to my surprise was the two other guys were couple and this guy (Allan) was a boyfriend to the girl who stereotyped me and the two remaining girls Dennie and her friend were single. I knew this as time went by when they were drinking, the other girl was the music selector. After, the song that was selected pushed them all to dance and couples were dancing, then Dannie looked at me and asked me whether I was interested in dancing when I told her it would be better when she taught me. She then laughed and came close to me and told me to stand up, she held my hands and directed me how the music playing was to be danced. During the dance I asked her a few questions and among those was the reason why many people were out at night at the beach today, she told me its because the summer is almost ending and sunrises are so beautiful as sunsets that was one of the reasons why they were sacrificing their sleep to see the beautiful moments. As we were dancing, many people came and joined us and the dancing was amusing, people were kissing each other and tightly holding each other. Dannie then looked at me and asked me why was I shying my eyes away from hers, I told her that I always get shy when I am doing something for the first time, then she asked me what it was. I then told her that I had never gotten a tight sweet dance like the one we were having at that time. She then told me that as the dance tends to the end, it becomes more interesting and intense, I was not getting what she said and immediately she told me to hold her by the waste using my two hands, and I should make it tight and close. I could not reject so I did what she asked me to and she held her two hands by my neck region and looked at me straight in the eyes and slowly she closed her eyes as she pulled me down slowly bending towards her and she slowly kissed me, and continued to kiss me once more. It was my first time to get such a romantic kiss, because she was feeling it and during the whole process she was closing her eyes and I also felt, it was really different from the kisses I had ever gotten. After a while she stood up and still closing her eyes, she told me to kiss her, I was afraid at that time but she then whispered in my ear that everyone was looking at us and once I don't do it I would get emclubrassed as well as she was to be ashamed. I was not afraid to kiss her but I was starting to get moody so I never wanted to continue with it but I had to, so I slowly pulled her much close and closed my eyes as I reached her lips and slowly kissed her and after I tightly hugged her and asked her whether she was satisfied. She then told me she was in moody moods at the moment. I told her I was in the same and I was sorry. She then told me people were all still kissing and she asked me to kiss her again. I told her I would like to sit down because I was so moody and I never wanted to get ashamed when everyone sits before us. She then held me by the had and took me to a place where she was sitting and she was trying to ask me whether I would try out doing something with her. I told her it would be my pleasure but it was not my intention, and I would like to respect her, she then told me she would like to atleast try it with an African and it was her chance then. I told her she was a little drunk and she needed to take some rest,and she told me she was sober, then at that time people said they were to go in the sea and swim as it was almost sun set. She then told me that she was going too and she would like me to join. I agreed and cold as it was, I removed my clothes and we went in the sea, but it was a little warm in the sea, and we started swimming. I was swimming and she told me that she would like to show me something, I approached her and she held my hands and started playing but then she after held her hands along my neck and approached closer and kissed me. I asked her what she was trying to do and she kept silent and looked at me and asked me whether I wont kiss her back. I was really moody and never wanted to also get ashamed and lose the chance, I kissed her back and she moved her hands secretly in the water and got hold of my wood. For sure I was so moody and she never wanted to leave the kiss, she told me that she wanted to do it at that time when I told her I could not because we had no protection. She then said I was scared, and

behaving childish. I told her we could go to my accommodation
and I was having protection there. She said she could not wait and
immediately we went off the sea and we walked a few minutes to
my accommodation. At the entrance, the security asked her
whether she had an ID, she showed it and we entered, reaching
the room, she was in a hurry to start when I told her I had to first
look for protection and she was getting angry because I was
making things so long. Good enough we had protection packs in
our bathrooms and I went back to her. She was looking at and I
was scared whether her moods had gone, but I approached her
and held her hand, she then closed her eyes and I knew she was
still in moods, I just continued. We had gone to watch the sunrise
but the sunrise watched us. We never knew when we got asleep,
just waking up and seeing the sun passing its rays through the
windows was the best thing we saw.

HOST day 2

In the morning, she woke up, and she was in a hurry telling me she was to be with her friends and she wanted to leave very fast. I told her to first take shower, then we could go have breakfast together then she could go. She agreed only to take shower and after that she went to her friends, I walked her towards the bus station and she promised to text when she reached. I also had to rush to the lecture which had started 30 minutes back. I entered the lecture hall and sat behind. This was the last lecture in the program and it was about The sustainable Tourist. I was in the lecture by body and my mind and soul was still in the night of the day before. It was my first engagement with a white lady and memorable, I kept on trying to remember what had happened in the night when I brought the protection and my mind was blowing out, make myself shy and smiling all the time. I got hold of my phone and opened Instagram asking Dennie whether she reached and she had left a message that I sleep badly. When I read it I even laughed and texted her to check whether she arrived to her friends and she never texted back immediately. My friend whom I had sat with in the behind seats asked me why I was opening my phone in the lecture hall yet I never did so ever since I came to the program. I was trying to pretend as if I was just checking my whatsApp messages but he told me that he saw me in the morning with a lady who was not part of the team and he was asking whether I knew her or I was just hooking up. I could not answer him but he insisted and I told her that I met her on the train we tool from Neubradenburg last two days. He was cool and then told me to check my phone maybe she had texted back. I asked him why was he saying so and how he knew I texted her not someone else. He then told me that he saw me writing a message and he knew that I was texting her because I asked her whether she had reached and she also had sent me a message that I had bad sleeping postures. I told him not to look into my phone again and he agreed. After I checked and she had replied by saying she had reached safely and she was going back her parents had called her and they were going to Netherlands for a family reunion. I was then feeling safe because she was safe but then I got hurt that she was leaving may be there would have had another time of meeting. After I send her a message that I was going to miss her she called me on Insta-video and I had to get out of the lecture hall and rush to the safe place and talked to her. She was persuading me to make a travel to the Netherlands but I told her I was to go back to India immediately and I was not to wait for more than a day, and I told her I would love to visit but I was on a tight schedule. We all said good bye and she told me to keep in touch of which I had not to deny it. Soon as I entered the lecture was ending and we were heading for lunch.

The afternoon of wandering.

After the lunch, I was perturbed because the following day my friends were leaving and I was the last to stay in the accommodation yet I was not having my own charger or even a universal plug thus I could not charge my phone or even use any of my devices. I decided to miss the ceremony of the afternoon which was giving feedback and awarding certificates for Sustain MV to all participants and recognising best participants as well. I decided to move in the city center to search for the universal plug or a charger for my phone which was European style. I went to the bus station and entered headed to the city centre, on reaching there I checked different electronic shops and all were not having the product I wanted. I was wandering from different shops and got tired till when I remembered that it could be in Greifswald. I called Alex and told him I wanted to meet him and he asked me the reason, I told him it was personal and I was on my way to Greifswald in the train. He agreed and told me to inform him a few minutes before the train reaches Greifswald. I rushed to the train station and luckily the next train was leaving in five minutes, I waited for it and boarded. It was just 30 minutes train drive to Greifswald. Before I reached the station in Greifswald, I called him and on reaching I met him standing at the bus station. He was happy to see me thinking I have some useful things to tell him yet I was in need of someone who knew the place to help me find what I needed. I told him I was looking for the plug which can allow me connect my USA-charge type to European. He then asked me whether I tried Stralsund shops and supermarkets and I told him, I did but I never found any. He said then we had to check all the electronic shops in Greifswald too and if we fail we can take a bus to the biggest shopping mall in Greifswald. I agreed, we started shop by shop wandering here and there. We checked the first six shops and then I asked him whether I had disturbed his schedule and he told me he was having no plans just in him room bored and watching movies. I told him I was heading back to my country two days after tomorrow and he was asking me why was I leaving early. I told him I was to go back for my college. We then went to the bus station and boarded for the supermarket, it was a little far from the old market and I told him I was going to be free from tomorrow afternoon till the next day evening and if he would want to show me around the place again it would be okay. Before he could agree he said, the transport charges will be high as the month of September would be starting and the 9eticket wont be in use any more. He would have loved to take me to many places and even the black forest. I told him that the next day he could come with the 9e ticket then once he arrives we use it to travel from the afternoon till the night when it gets done and maybe he could sleep at my accommodation and he will go the next day back to his place. He hesitated and he said he would think about it. We had finally reached the supermarket and he told me he always enters while running and he did the same, I also followed and we climbed till the third floor where the electronics and gadgets were sold in different shops and cubicles. We started from the first one to the last one and they all had non and one person told us that they get exhausted very quickly more so during the summer season because many tourists come to buy them. I asked him when the next shipment will and he said once the demand is high they will bring. I was almost crying till when I asked Alex to ask them whether I would get my phone charger and they had it so I bought one and it was time we headed back. Before we started our journey back, Alex told me he would never leave this supermarket without taking some tea from his favourite tea shop, I agreed and we went to the shop, he asked me whether I would like some tea and when I looked at the price of one cup, I was getting scared, I told him I would take when I was back at my accommodation, he disagreed and ordered for me as well. We took the tea and I was trying to make some conversation when I saw he was not in moods and I asked him what was the problem, he told me he agrees to come to my accommodation in the afternoon the next day, I told him if he never wanted to come or having a busy schedule he would leave it because I was just in need of someone who knows the place we just enjoy the travel using the 9eticket before it expire and it would help me add on my Germany experience. He said he was supposed to work but because I was in need of company he was still thinking what to tell his boss. I told him to leave it and head to his work because I might make him lose his job yet I was just not meaning it. He said he will let me know before 9 AM in the morning the following day. I agreed and we continued with the tea, it was very good, tasty, fresh made and flavoured with vanilla. After the tea he paid and we went back to the bus station, on reaching he asked me whether I was going at that time back to Stralsund or I was staying longer, I told him I was going back and asked him whether he had other option. He told me to go with him to his parent's place and then I could go back. I told him I left my friends in the last ceremony and I ran away looking for the electronic device because most of them were to leave the next day and yet they were the ones who were helping me to charge my phone and my laptop so I had to look for it before it was too late. He agreed and boarded with me another bus to the train station. When I reached I hugged him and thanked him so much that he accepted to help me once again. I told him I was grateful for him kind heart. I boarded back to Stralsund and on reaching everything was done and my certificate was given to my Rwandan friend and by that time people had gone outing and drinking. I tested the charger I bought by plugging my phone and once it was charging I left it on and took a shower, prepared my dinner and sat on my bed thinking how the day tomorrow will be and after when all my friends were gone and the program was done. I remembered that my bus ticket to Berlin Airport, was scheduled for the day next, and I had to change it before it was late. I asked my Rwandan friend to text me once he was in his room so as he could help me do the reschedule. But I had two plans either to get a hotel booking in Berlin or reschedule but once I checked the hotel booking in Berlin and the cheapest was more than 50e I remained with one option and had to wait. I contacted Elisabeth about the accommodation whether I will be allowed to stay an extra day and she told me I was to be charged 35e which was also kinda high, Later when I told her my situation she agreed to talk with the manager and she told me to get back to me the next day. After a few hours, my friend from Rwanda had come to his room and he called, he had bought some dinner and asked me to join him, during the process he helped me change my bus ticket and I paid him with cash. He also handed me my certificate and we called it off. After a few hours, I was asleep and waking up was the next day.

CHAPTER EIGHT

Closing Sustain MV

The next day I woke up very late, I prepared myself and rushed for breakfast. I had forgotten that the 9e ticket had ended working and my friends had gotten tickets for the closing ceremony and since I was absent I had not got. I messaged in the group to know how I could find my way to the ceremony and Frank messaged back that i had to go and grab a bus to the town center of which I had no ticket and he told me that the bus drivers could sale tickets at 1.2e which works for one time drive. I went and did as Frank instructed and I was a few minutes late before the opening of the ceremony. The ceremony was organised in a the Town hall beautiful will large crystal chandeliers, on every hair was a microphone and screens were displaying everything that was taking place. Drinks were plenty at self-service basis, snacks and fruits were also in play. We were all wearing the outfits we thought were the best and delegates from the local, central and higher governments in Germany were presented. Professors, and Sustain MV organising team was present to elucidate the program and its fruits to the men and women in power. They were also allowed to speak to us about the future of Sustain MV and their roles both in and out of offices. We were also allowed to ask them a few questions and they had to answer accordingly. The ceremony was short and informative. We took farewell pictures with different people and had fun for the last time as some of our friends were leaving just after the ceremony. After the closure, Elisabeth informed us to have lunch with them at the gazetted place and we followed. We all sat together and had our last meal and drink as Sustain MV team 2022 version. Some people had started going for their buses and others for train. Many people went immediately and a few went hours after. I was the last one left who was to go the day after. Before I left the dinner, Elisabeth told me the manager had accepted me to stay till the next day without payment and once I was leaving I had to leave the keys to the reception and sign-out.

The Afternoon alone.

When I went out of the dinner, I checked my phone and no missed call, no message just date and time. I moved slowly to the Town church and sat at the stairs, scrolling through my news-fees on Facebook. Suddenly I received an call from Alex that he could not make it that day and his manager never accepted him to leave. I told him it was okay and officially I was saying goodbye to him because the day after I was to travel to Berlin and then go back to my country. I then started the journey back to the accommodation but when I was about to board the buy, I remembered that I had not toured the locale where I was and decided to trek back to the accommodation. I walked slowly observing the different laces, architecture and how the locale was organised with each street having a well labelled note and each station was clearly visible. Fresh air and beautiful flowers across the sides of the road and on the houses. I then passed at the beach and met an African who stared at me and I went close to him, he asked me where I was heading and I told him I was just wandering around and opted to swim, but I wanted to ask him whether the water was fresh or salty but then I feared. He told me it was okay, he had also come to sunbath and swim as well. So I decided to join him and we removed our clothes and stayed in briefs, jumped into the water and started swimming. During the process he was asking me my country, where I was staying in the locale and what course I was doing with many other questions. I told him I was for a short program in Germany and I had just ended the same day, so I was having some free time alone before I depart for Berlin and back home the next day. He then told me he was Kenny and he was from Nigeria and was taking his masters of science in Nano-engineering and was in the nearby university in Stralsund. After some time we went off the waters and I was feeling hungry, he told me he was hungry and he had prepared food back in his place we could grab it together. I did not deny as his place was not far from the beach side, we walked a few minutes and reach his place, he opened and it was really looking nice as a hotel I stayed in yet he was a student in university accommodation. I was feeling so much in love to study my masters in Europe. He served the food, fried rice and chicken, as you know Nigerian foods are so sweet. When I finished eating I was feeling sleepy and I wanted to go back to my accommodation then Kenny told me to just take a quick sleep in his bed once I am okay I would just go back to my place as well. I laid down on his bed and slept. I have a challenge that I cant sleep in full clothes and the only comfortable clothes I sleep in are briefs or completely off clothes, so when I woke up this Kenny dude was sleeping behind me cuddling me but because we were all asleep and it was the door knock that woke me up and I woke him up to go check who was calling him, I never wanted to fume. He went to the door and the next thing I was hearing was he was telling someone I never saw but heard a masculine voice that he could come back after one hour and I though it was the supervisor or friends who wanted to take him somewhere but because I was inside he never wanted to go which was understandable because I was a stranger in his house. The person at the door insisted and trying to enter he saw me by the mirror reflection and the next thing was quarrelling as Kenny was cheating and even reached to an extent of bring a bitch in his house, such stuff and I was in total mess. He tried to calm down this other dude but all was in vain, and he angrily walked away. When Kenny came inside I asked him whether that was his boyfriend and he said yes, but he never expected him to be back by that time. I told him why he never let him in because we were not lovers or doing anything bad, and he said that he already saw me not even wearing clothes and thought we were doing nasty stuff. I asked him whether he had intentions of doing that stuff with me, and he agreed and I frankly told him I was not into it and I also told him that I would also explain why he was cuddling me when I was sleeping and he agreed. I told him I wanted to leave his place and he should find a way of talking to his friend or boyfriend, such that they can continue their relationship as I was just a pawn in a wrong square. I left the place wondering and hurrying to reach my place maybe to get more rest and even take a shower. I reached my accommodation and took a warn shower, then opened my fridge and found my burger which was for yesterday, placed it in the microwave and crushed the coffee beans, then served my self dinner. I sat on my bed and opened my phone and had no message at all but I had a missed called from Alex. I called him back and he said he was in Stralsund and he called while I was not picking. I was surprised, then I asked him where he was and he told me he was at Kneiper nord bus station sitting, I went out and picked him up. I took him to my room and made him coffee. I asked him why was he risking to come late in the night. He told me he wanted to say goodbye in a good way. I was happy to see him, and just sad that he came at night, so I asked him whether he was planning to stay for the night such that we can make the tour of the place tomorrow as my bus was in the late afternoon at 4 PM. He agreed he was to stay for the night and I asked him whether he was hungry or he was fit and he told me he had eaten dinner once the bus dropped him at the town center. I ordered for towels and extra blanket for him and he went and took a shower. He had his small back pack containing his laptop and some extra clothes for tomorrow, after shower he tied the towel on and came, I was not even frightened or even shy at him because he was my fellow man and I had been in such associations before in high schools where we never even minded about some stuff once we were same sex, we gave no thought of other stuff. So when he was about to wear his boxers, he tried to shy away of which I realised he was not from the same pot I was cooked in when I was growing up. I pretended to be on my phone and when he was done he jumped into the bed and started asking me whether I was fine with him staying or it affected me. I told him I was fine and with his presence I felt not bored and more so he was making me lively like having my brother. I was tired and wanted to sleep, so I laid first and slept, before I reached the extreme sleep stage, I heard his hands touching my chest and lips and I never wanted to wake up because I was tire, and even thought it was a dream. Kisses also felt like dreams because I could get such dreams when I am being kissed but what made me wake up was feeling the softness and warmness of the mouth on my motor. I woke up but never opened my eyes so wide for him to notice and I never shock but I left him to do what he wanted, more so I was enjoying it besides the fact that it was from a man and he was doing it so good. He then came back to the mouth for more kissed and he saw me looking at him. He felt shy and ashamed, I was really in need of finishing the process of boiling the oil he had started and just kissed him back, but stupidly I was looking for the breasts as usually used to women, I left that and he just went down and continued to roll his tongue on my motor. He then went onto his bag and got some slippery substances and protection, I was just watching because it was a new field and something I had never done and even thought of doing it. I cant tell what he did but the next thing I remember was he was riding me and kissing me at the same time. All I wanted was to pour the cooked oil and sleep. He did it in a way he seemed to be enjoying and I was groaning just like a buffalo being scratched in the back. In a few minutes he had make a mess on my stomach and unfortunately my oil had just started pouring and he just slept over me for about two minutes. He then went off and removed the rubber, and I told him we had to bathe. He asked me why and I told him, because he had already finished when he came in but then I explained to him that the norms of my religion it is a must once such things happen. He agreed and we did bathe and coming back to bed he was happy and slept his head on my chest, as his hands were still infiltrating my genitals. I was not happy but scared and asking myself how I could have done such a thing. But I had not to react because it was done and all I had to do was sleep and find a new day tomorrow. By the time I laid down my thoughts to sleep he had already slept.

The last Eagle to leave the nest.

The morning of the next day, as usual I woke up earlier than Alex and took shower, prepared myself a cup of coffee with some bread toasts and omelets. I then opened my phone and saw my aunt had called and due to time differences she called deep in the night so I never picked her. I decided to call her but in UAE it was already night and she never picked. Just a few minutes Alex woke, I told him we were late and yet we had to roam around the cities from Stralsung to Greisfswald and Rostock. I told him to fresh-up and get some breakfast then we could start the Roam. Before he went to the bathroom, he asked me whether I was angry with him. I told him I was not and also asked him why would he think like that. He told me that he drove me to do something at night that I would never do and he thought I was angry at him. I told him everything was fine and I was not angry at him, but rather I told him to hurry we had many cities to cover in less time. He then hurriedly went into the bathroom and took a shower. In a few minutes he was out and went to the kitchen to make himself breakfast, then came near where I was sitting and started taking his breakfast. I started a simple jazz with him asking him whether he knew well the places we were going to, and he was shyly answering minus looking in my eyes and even he was not comfortable, I sensed it because I was wearing just my shorts and vest which was making him not fine to look at me. I then asked him whether I was making him feel not well and he said I was making him moody, so I got a shirt on and told him to hurry as we were getting late. I wore my grey sweeter-pants and winter sweeter on because it was a little chilly for me, and he just wore summer shorts and tight shirt, he was looking good while I was looking like an Eskimo. We started our journey of free roam by taking a train to Greifswald, which was about half an hour, in the train we were sitting just next to each other and some couple in front of us started asking him questions in Germany language, they talked like for 5 minutes and then he looked at me and laughed and I asked him why he was laughing and he told me that he lied to the couple that we were dating. I got furious but I never showed him that I was angry and I asked him why would he do that and perhaps he would have told me about the conversation because it involved me as well. He then told me that it was all fine as most people in Germany like asking such questions when they see two people of foreign origins together. In about half an hour, we had reached Greifswald and exited the train. We went to the bus station and I asked him whether he had an I dear where we were going and he told me he had no idea but once we could reach the town center we could decide where to go. I was okay with and as soon as the bus came we entered and went to the town center. Reaching, we I told him I was having a plan and once he asked me to go through it I told him that since all the three places had beaches, and it was a weekend, I suggested we visit each beach for about one hour and swim for like 30 minutes then go to another city. He was so exited and asked me whether I had swimming clothes when I told him I never had because I had just gotten the idea at the time we were in Greifswald. He suggested we buy some swimming costumes and head to the beach. I told him I was not in capacity to spend any money because I was still having another journey to move through. He agreed and told me that we go and buy the costumes as he would pay. We looked for the supermarket nearby and entered, reaching the costumes section they were very expensive and I told him I was to get a boxer brief which I can wear instead of swimming costume, He bought his costume and I bought the brief and light shorts. We then went out and hurried to the bus station to the nearest destination tot he beach, and once we reached the pier, we head loud music down the beach side as holiday makers had already started enjoying and weekend moods were in higher concentrations.

The Great Roam

Soon as we heard the loud music, Alex told me we had to run and I had no option because immediately he said, he started running to the beach and I followed, since it was peak summer, the weather was sunny and we met very many people at the beach. When we reached, we secured our spot, and changed to the beach moods and clothes. We had no towels and yet we wanted to swim, no oil or cream but we had agreed on swimming so we had to do it. Immediately we changed our clothes, we went to the sea and entered the waters, it felt so cold at first and I was just walking fearing to get fully submerged in the water. Alex splashed the water to me and I looked at him with an angry face, I saw it in his eyes that he had gotten scared, I immediately turned to play mode, I splashed it back to him and many people joined the play. We swum and enjoyed because we were not alone anymore but we joined the crowd we met at the beach. I will say most of them were young teenagers and a few people whore were beyond 20s but those were swimming alone and because I was with Alex who was a teenager, I was among the crowd group. Mixed, males and females we were all enjoying. Swimming competitions, splash plays, diving plays, water volley ball, and many others. we thought we would do the swimming for about 30 minutes, it took almost an hour, in about 45 minutes of all the swimming, many people had gotten tired and people started to swim in pair and others with their friends while a few left the water and went for sun bathing. Alex came close to me and asked me whether he could cuddle with me in the water, I told him never and he was disappointed as I saw it in his eyes. I then told him, it would not have been a problem but the beach was a public place and he told me we were getting late for the next beach as it was high time we left the water. As we moved out, few of the boys saw us trying to shake the water from our bodies and they called us, we approached them and they told us they had some good places for sun bathing, something I had never done before and even never thought of doing. I told Alex we were going to be late, then he said it would just take 30 minutes and in the next 30 minutes we were to take a train to Rostock so we were not to worry unto anything. We went to the spot the boys had called us in. We found many boys sunbathing but they were all naked and had hanged their underies/ briefs and costumes for drying. I was scared and I told Alex as I was not going to do such a thing. He told me I could just lay down in the sand the way I wanted as being nude was not a must. We laid in the sun and Alex had gone with the custom of being nude, and I rejected it. Because I was looking in the sky, it was so bright to my eyes that I decided to close them. In a few minutes, I heard someone touching my thighs and Abs region, I never took it badly I thought it was Alex because I knew he was having that moody feeling when ever I was half naked and close to him. But situation got worse when the person went further to touch my wood and trying to make be become moody. At that time I said, "Alex stop, I told you I cant do this again. Just understand my point." The person stopped and Alex tapped me on the shoulder and I looked at him, he then asked me what I was talking about because he was not doing anything to me as he was also sunbathing and had closed his eyes. I wondered who it was but felt so bad that I was rude at Alex who never thought of such a thing. I saw he was angry and held him by the head, and he turned towards me and asked me what I was doing. I then told him I was sorry. He then quickly kissed, and hugged me. During the process he climbed over me and looked at me in a romantic and sexy way. I rolled him down and told him we had to go catch the next bus, but he had almost dragged me to moody styles and because he was nude, he had become moody already. Good enough people were not even minding because even we saw some other people who were blowing each other by the time we went to the spot for sunbathing. I left him and went to our spot, removed the wet pant and wore a dry one then sat waiting for him. He came in an angry face and sat down, he then looked at me and asked me why I never liked him, whether he was not looking nice or he was not being nice to me. I told him he was my friend and I liked him but I was not into loving men or even having affair with them even though what had happened last night, we had some enjoyment but it was not that I was into such stuff. I then told him I was sorry for not being who he wanted me to be. He then looked at me and asked me to just give him some good last moments of happiness with him because we were never going to meet again and being that I was not in the men loving men group, I told him I never knew how to pretend to give him the happiness he wanted but I promised him to try. I then told him I was sorry and hugged but this time he made me stay in the hug for about a minute. After that, we hurried to wear and remove the sand from our body then rushed to the train station. I was about 6 hours to my bus to Berlin and we had to cover more two cities. We entered the bus and headed for the train station. We almost reached when the rain was about to leave because we were the last people to board. We entered and seats were all occupied, we stool and after some few minutes we go seats from the people who were exiting at the near by station. We sat on opposite chairs this time and we were looking at each other, shyly he asked me why I was looking at him and I told him he was a good boy. He then asked me why I said so. I told him that besides the differences we had, he made me enjoy Germany and was a good company. He then asked me whether I was having anyone I loved back where I came from. I told him that I had and he was silent. After some time we reached Rostock.

Rostock Monument Square Performances.

As we went off the train station in Rostock, we read the map and it was a long way from the train station to the beach. We were even still having some small disputes among each other and we never talked till we went out and walked for about 5 minutes. As we moved, I asked him whether he knew where we were going but he never answered. I asked him whether he would talk to me again or not. He then told me he was still feeling angry because he rushed for things. I told him he was not supposed to blame himself and I was okay with all that he as doing and I enjoyed being with him. He then told me to atleast hold his hand as we walk, which I never rejected and immediately he started being joyous and normal again. as we moved towards the city center at the monumental ground, we encountered on-street performances including street magic, music and acrobatics and he decided that we could stay and watch for about 30 minutes at the Rostock monument square. We watched the performances, Alex was enjoying more the magic tricks and when we went to observe nearer, the magician spotted us and called us, I looked behind and he again said to us that, "I mean you who had looked behind" I got fear and Alex pushed me to the front, then the magician told the two of us to join. Me and Alex were put into the magic trick. The trick was a about mind reading. He asked us some questions about our relationship and how we met with many other stuff. after that he told us to hold hands as we was going to extract one thought from my head and send it to Alex's head who will say it to the public and once it was correct, his trick will be valid. He then said since we are friends, there is possibility that Alex already knows my thought at the moment but he the magician doesn't know thus he was to write it down on a piece of paper and after Alex says the thought, he would show his paper to prove his trick. We all agreed and he started the trick. He said some enchantments and hypnotic stuff then after he told us to open our eyes. I was sure Alex can never know my thought and I had belief that magic is fallacy. He then asked Alex to say anything he had got from my brain. Alex was scared and confused because it was his first time to be in magic tricks same as I was. He then said that I was going to miss him when I leave him today as I go to Berlin and back to my home place. I was so socked and I never believed it, but the magician revealed his answer and it was "I am going to miss you, Alex. You were like a brother to me". This moment blew my mind because it was the thought I never thought anyone could know. We then went off the stage and the magician was given a big applause. Alex then hugged me and held my hand so tight and told me, he thought I was lying to him and I never liked him. After that performance, we went to the hitting music and we danced, after about 30 minutes, I was feeling so hungry, I told Alex we had to eat lunch and he led me to the nearby restaurant and we got a table for two. Immediately we sat some teenagers approached and started asking us some questions and one of them asked whether I had come to visit Alex, I told then I had come for my research but then Alex was the first person I met who was so hospitable and loving as he helped me in many things and he tried to make me enjoy Germany. Then one of the girls asked me whether I was taking him as a friend, lover or just another stranger. I told her, he was my brother and I loved him so much. Then as they were bringing more questions, Alex talked with them in German language and they went away. The waiter brought our food and he started eating. Alex asked me why I was not staying for long because he was getting attached to me so much. I told him I could not because I had to finish some things in my College and back home. After lunch we headed to the acrobatics show and we enjoyed for about 30 minutes when I told him that we had to go to the next city as my bus travel was near. I had only a few hours to the bus journey. We then headed to the bus station and went to the train station. This time we were going to Stralsund the last stop for our free roam. In the train, Alex asked me whether I will really miss him and I told him I was going to miss him so much and if I could show it he would agree but it was hard for me to show it. In about one hours we had reached the train stop at Stralsund and we approached the bus stop. I told him we had to go to the beach before it was too late and then we could come back early and I refresh and get read for the journey to Berlin. We hurried and in a few minutes we were at the sandy path to the beach.

Stralsund Beach.

We moved slowly to the beach and what was at the beach was like going to the club when you don't drink. Every spot was filled with couples and here came the two single men coming in with no babes. Alex then held my hand and we passed via the first four couples and got a spot in between the fifth and the sixth couple. Many people we in the water swimming and a few were sunbathing while some were in romantic talks, kisses and even wearing each other sunscreen. No one was minding us, and we got prepared for swimming. Before we went to the water, one pass by gay couple saw us and they came to us. They told us that we were strong to start an interracial relationship at a young age and they were certain it will last. I was about to tell them, that we were not dating or lovers but then I decided to just keep myself low of words because I knew the truth and I was not going to be in the place for days. Alex held my hand as we walked into the water and once we reached he started splashing the water onto my body, I also did the same. I just decided to act stupidly and just make his last moments with me memorable and joyful. We then started swimming heading to the crowd of teenagers who were in the water. He then stopped and asked me to have a good mature swimming, I told him I never knew how it looked like. He then told me he would lead. I told him it was okay and he came close to me and made his body touch mine, held me by the neck and asked me to hold his waste. then he twisted his legs on my lower body and looked in my eyes, I asked him what he was doing and he never said anything. After a while I heard some crowd voice shouting, "Kiss him!, Kiss him!..." I was shocked and he told me not to look at them but just do what they say or not. I was fearing and lowered my, kissed him and in the background the crowd was clapping and shouting, "That is awesome" and going wild. After doing that I dived with him in the water and we swum under to another place. We continued to swim and a couple approached us and unluckily they were not speaking English so Alex talked with them and after he told me they were asking him how he met and whether he thought I was the perfect partner for him. I also asked him what he told them and he said he told them that he had met me from the tourist center and we were just loving each other just for a while because I had to go back. I just could not do anything and I was just quiet. We continued to enjoy the water and playing the two of us. Alex then was becoming so moody because I had granted him access to myself and I was also trying to give him the good time he wanted, so he started to make actions to my wood and touching my chest and Abs region with deep compassion and desire. He did it for like four times and I noticed he had become wood hard, I asked him whether he was comfortable or he was not feeling well. He then looked at me and pushed my head in the water when I came back he hugged me and I was not seeing well because my face was covered with water so he kissed me and told me, we had to go because my bus was near to departure time. He told me he was hard wood and could not get out of the water he might get ashamed so he asked me to lift him. So I did lift him from my front and he was hugging me and once I reached him at the spot we were staged, he said he wanted to still stay on my body for a while. This scene from the far looked like two people in deep love lifting each other and talking sweet-nothings. He looked in my eyes and told me to guess what he was thinking I told him I never use assumptions so I could not see it. He then said we had to go else I would be late for the bus. We hurried and wore our clothes back and as we passed by the beach shop we bought some fish burgers and french fries. the distance to my accommodation from the beach was about 4 minutes walk. We reached and at that time I was having less than an hour to bus departure. Once we entered, I told him we were supposed to bath before we eat the burgers. He agreed and I went to the bath room first, I had forgotten to lock the door to the bathroom and he also entered and said once we bath together we could save more time as we had less than an hour. As soon as he entered the bathroom, he came close to my body and got hold of my wood, then looked at me and closed his eyes. I was frightened, and he intimately hugged me and moved his head towards my nipples and started to disturb them. I was so shocked, frightened and fearing what I was going to do again. He went further and reached my Umbilicus region and at that time I was hard-wood as an iron club. His hand never left the hard-wood and he came back to my head and looked at me. In my freezing position I was like a dummy, he romantically kissed me and I was out of options. He then told me that it was not my fault but his fault and he told me to forgive him, he had just lost control. As he stepped out of the shower area, I pulled him by the soapy hand and h bumped onto my body, and I lifted him up. This time it was me driving, I kissed him and he could not hesitate to make the weird noise. He then pushed me to the wall and knelt down, for a blow. I pulled him up and put him in the middle of the shower area, flowing water onto our bodies, we were kissing and it was not enough for all of us because we were all at higher levels and if we just left it in the shower it will not have lowered the highness we had, I opened the door to the bathroom and took him to the bed side. That is where the whole remaining process ended.

After about one hour, we had finished everything and even took shower. But I was sure that the bus had left me and the other options I had was to book for a train ticket to Berlin. He was warming the burgers in the oven and preparing tea. I looked again on my ticket and I was still having more two hours. I remembered that I always claim two hours of waiting time to buses and flights hence I was still having two hours. I told him and he was happy, he then came with the burgers and we ate them and he asked me whether I was in mood to do it again as the farewell. I told him it was enough and I had to organise for the bus journey. After the snack we ate, he helped me organise and check out as well.

Berlin, One last look

When we checked out, the bus station FlixBus was far from my accommodation and I had to take intra-town buses to reach to it. I asked Alex whether he would go with me to the bus station, he told me he will leave once the bus I am boarding to Berlin Leaves. We then moved together to the bus station and got to the bus station. In the bus, he was holding me tight and asking me whether I will ever come back to Germany. I told him I may never come back because even coming was a chance and I will be finishing my studies the year to come so I was to go back to my native country and start another life. He laid his head on my woollen winter jacket at the shoulder side and told me he had a very wonderful and amazing experience with me and all the moments will stay in his memories forever. I could not say anything because I knew I would never come back, he then asked me to always keep checking on him on Instagram. I agreed and he gave me his handle name. After a while we reached the bus stop which was near to the station. We were about 30 minutes early and we sat in the waiting place, we were the only two people in the waiting area bench. He told me to wrap my hand along his shoulder and comfort him because he was feeling sad and lonely. He then passed his hand beneath the shirt I was wearing and was touching my chest and Abs region. I just never wanted to make his last moment hell and I left him do the things he wanted. After a while I heard his hand sloping down my pubic region and he got hold of my wood, I cant describe what he was doing and how he was felling but he seemed to be settled and comfortable. He looked in my eyes one last time and told me that he would like to sit on my laps cross-legged for the last time. I told him it was fine and he did. He then started to stare at me and asked me to do something, I told him I never knew what to do and he told me to close my eyes. Once I did, he of-course kissed and was really taking it to the next level suddenly the bus arrived and I was the only one to be picked at that particular station. I stopped him from the kissing competition and told him it was time I left. He rolled my bag to the bus and as I was about to enter i told him goodbye and he called me to go back for a second, and once I went close to him, he held me by the neck with his two hands and told me to hold him the right way, I also held him by the waist and he then kissed and said,"Goodbye, have a nice journey." I thanked him very much for being with me and for being so kind and hospitable. Then I let go of him, and entered the bus, I sat just a few chairs from the entrance close to the window and I saw him stand till the bus passed him and he waived the last bye to me and I did the same.

Rolling into Berlin.

The bus journey took about three hours, in the bus were toilets, WiFi and even on-board screen showing both the map of the journey and the weather updates in transition. I actually started missing Alex for his company and hospitality he showed. As the bus drove for about one hour, it went to a new station to pick up some other people as well as to give us room for refreshing and buying some edibles. I never knew that the toilets were in the bus so I went to the driver and showed him using google-translate what I wanted and he directed me in the bus. I went in and was wondering how the bus had the toilet embedded in it. At this station we spent less than an hour and we were back on travel again. At the station we picked two teenagers both were boys and one of them sat next to me and I have a habit of initiating conversation once someone is next to me but if the person cuts the conversation off, I don't talk to them any-more even though they initiate it again. I said Hi to him and luckily he replied, and he was a good talkative person so he started asking me about my whereabouts and other stuff. As we discussed he told me he was going in Berlin to see his friends and then head to the Berlin city tour and other stuff. I told him I was heading for my flight even though it was not for that day but I was tired of the city I was so I decided to head to Berlin to stay near the airport and make a good tour of the Capital of Germany. He was so happy and told asked me the hotel name I was going to take accommodation from for the night and the day tomorrow till my flight. I told him I was to book it once I reached in Berlin. He asked me the station I was to be dropped by the bus and I just showed him my bus ticket. On seeing the drop point he said his drop point was the same and he showed me on his phone. I asked him whether he will help me get a cheap hotel for the night since I never knew the language and I was not having a good connection to make booking as well as my money was in cash only. He then told me that I needed not to book one because he booked for a whole week and I could go stay with him for the night and I leave the next day to the airport.

I asked him how much it would be and he told me I will just use the money to buy myself dinner and breakfast in the morning. I had got a new friend and sorry I never told you his name before but he was called Neil. He was really talkative and he talked the whole remaining two hours of the journey till when we left the bus. On reaching the station, I was looking at the beauty of the City. This time I was not at the train station, I was in the middle of the city. Neil called his friends and they told him he could meet them at certain club they were heading there for the night enjoyment. He then told me we had to walk just a few minutes to his hotel where he had made booking. We reached the hotel, it was so elegant and beautiful. The lobby alone was so catchy and free fruits and sweets were placed at almost every corner for all the guests to enjoy. We went to check in and he told the desk that he would like to check in with his guest for a night and they asked for our IDs and the keys were given to him. After some time we were called when our luggage was shifted to our room by the boys working in the rooms as service boys. Room 314 was the booked room as the first number indicted the floor and the last two numbers were for the exact room. Keys were digital as cards and code locks were on the doors as well as biometrics. We entered the room and it was fancy and so elegant with a large round bed. The bathroom was so big with bath-tab inside and shower heads on the other side. A large mirror at the dressing place and room perfumes, a glass round table with a glass shapeless jar of wine was on top with red-rose wine and glasses were made to lean against the wine glass. The woollen carpet at the floor with fluffy wool and beautiful colourful designs and welcome note at the entrance. As we entered, Neil told me he would want to take a shower first and he was like a person used to such kind of life, but I was in wonders. Just after a few minutes, a service boy came and rung the bell asking if he would be useful in case we needed anything. He had also brought the towels and snacks for the evening with tea and coffee. I asked him to place everything on the table and told him to wait a little while might be that Neil would need something. In a few minutes Neil was out of the bathroom and I also decided to take a bath in the tab, I swear to god it was my first elegant bath tab bathe and I was feeling so relaxed. I never knew what happened after but the next thing I hear was Neil calling me that I had taken long in the bathroom. It seemed I had slept since I was comfortable in the tab and submerged. He then asked me to go with him to meet his friends at the club, I immediately told him that I was not a person of drinking and he insisted that I would drink soda and he just wanted my company and showbiz to his friends that he had gotten a stranger. I agreed and we got prepared, went out of the room and as we lowered down to the ground floor, I saw Neil wink at the boy room service and I remembered the boy by face. It was no biggie for me, I was just a person being helped with the room to stay for a night.

What happens in Rome .....

We went to the bus station and boarded a bus, about five minutes, we went out and headed to the club, I never had been in a club like the one we entered in, Neil approached a section where his friends were drinking from and he introduced me to them, they were a little older than him and almost all of them were in their late 20s except one boy who was in about Neil's age. I never wanted to go further and deeper with everything, I just said to them it was nice meeting them and one of them whose name I got to know as Matthew told me to sit down and make order for the drink. I told him Neil knows what I will drink and he immediately told him to get it, basing on the expression Neil did when he was told, it showed me that Matthew was the leader of their gang. They got me an iced coca-cola and all buzzed with beers and other expensive alcoholic drinks. They talked a lot of things and I saw one of the waiters in the club winking at Neil as the he did to the room-service boy. I just noticed it and never wanted to know what it meant and what they were doing. In few minutes, Neil excused himself and said he was going to the toilet for a piss. Others were drinking and asking me silly questions as I answered because I had no one to talk to. Neil then came back after about fifteen minutes and, I kept my eyes at the entrance to the toilet to see who gets out next within the next five minutes, as suspected the waiter whom I saw winking walked out and he was happy and shying away. The challenging part came when music was tunes to a beat that almost everyone knew and people decided to roll to the dance floor to dance and everyone including Neil was heading there. I never knew dancing and even never wanted to mix in a bunch of people who were under the influence of alcohol. Neil pulled me to the dance floor and told me to dance anything and if a girl comes and wants to dance I should not hesitate. On the dance floor, shouting and jumping was the most done action, I also did the same. Just after a few minutes of jumping and shouting, I suddenly knocked a young beautiful black girl and she looked at me and asked me whether I was enjoying the dance.// I was surprised and blushing to see her and even the question she asked me. I softly told her I was enjoying the dance and she told me she wanted to have some more drinks if I was interested to join her. I told her it was fine and we went to the counter and she ordered for drinks, I told her as I was not drinking alcoholic drinks and I asked for water. We talked and she told me she was called Angela from New-York and she had come for summer trip tour in Europe. She further told me that Germany was her last European country for the summer trip and within four days she was to go back to USA. I asked her whether she has come alone or with friends. She told me she had come with friends and they were having some male friends dancing except her. She then asked about me and I narrated to her my story and she asked whether I was going back to India or home country. I told her I was heading back to India the next day. She then told me she wanted to use a bathroom, and she went. I was seated and waiting for her, after like ten minutes she was not coming back and I decided to check where she went in the bathroom, when I reached the bathroom she was there leaning against the sink smoking cigarette and she said to me that she thought I was an amateur and I wont follow her. I never knew what she meant but I reached where she was and she lit off the cigarette and asked me whether I has a rubber or not. I was surprised and told her, I never had one. She then told me why I came in a club minus a rubber, its was a risky move I took. Luckily in Germany almost in all enjoyment places, rubbers are free and on every counter. So in my confused state thinking too much, she went out of the wash-room area and I thought she got disappointed and went away. I was stuck and thinking a lot. I was in fear and frightened mood, my brain was telling me that it was a bad move not to move with rubber but my heart was telling me it was a good thing to do because I was not in the club for such things. As I strengthened my self to get out and wait for Neil to come back from the crazy dance floor, Angela came back with the rubber and rapidly pulled me to one of the toilets and with no hesitation, she kissed me and I tried to tell her to stop, she could not and she just said one thing, "Please be silent, this is a lady's wash-room if they hear your voice it will be bad for you." I kept silent and she continued the process, took off her blouse and pulled my T-shirt and rolled it over my head. She then massaged my chest and nipples, I never knew where the fear went and then turned on with high volts. I was wearing my sweater-pant which she just pulled down to half the legs and then opened the rubber, put it on and the remaining process was self paced. In not more than 20 minutes, both the players were looking forward to be leaving the pitch. Immediately we were at the climax, two ladies entered and I was still groaning in deep exhalation voice when she blocked my mouth and she slowly laid her head on my shoulder till the ladies refreshed and went away. She then got off and I removed the rubber, to the trash and we went out. She then told me she was going back to the dance floor again as she had to meet her friends. I told her it was okay as I was heading back to the hotel to take some rest because it was a tiresome night. She then winked at me and told me, to have a good night. I smiled and waved slowly to her as she went. On moving to the place Neil and the friends were seated before, Neil was waiting for me and once I arrived, he told me we had to go rest enough as he and his friends were having some long day the next day. I told him I was sorry to delay him and he told me it was all fine and we went out of the club and took a bus to the hotel again. Reaching I told him I would want to stay at the Lobby for some time and I would be in the room after half an hour. He agreed and went up, I stayed in the lobby thinking of what had happened that time in the Club and I was both worried and happy tried to search on the risks of such actions. The fear I had was so intense but the joy I had was also much. I went to the fruits basket and got some fruits and before I sat, one of the room-service boys approached me and asked whether I was okay. I told him I was fine and later asked him whether it was fine for me to talk with him in private. He accepted and told me it would be better in the room I booked. I asked him why and he told me that most bosses do like that and they get the happiness they want as well as the information they need. I asked him whether my friends in the room 314 was one of the bosses he had once known to have reservations here. He told me that he was a regular boss in the hotel. The boy then excused himself and told me he would be happy to pass-by my reserved room and we talk as I requested. I told him I will then call him once I was in the room. I was shocked by the little I got to know and decided to go in the room to sleep such that the next day I head to the airport for my flight. Reaching the room number, Neil had closed it and I rung the bell for him to open and he was not opening, I rung again after two minutes, and he came on the door and looked through the door lens saw it was me, he opened and I entered. I never asked him anything but I told him I would just take a bath and sleep. When I went in the room deeper, I saw the room-service boy seated in the chair with no trousers on but I just never talked anything. I went to the bathroom and after a while I went away from the bathroom and wore a towel. I found Neil seated on the bed and he told me whether I was mad at him. I told him why would he ask me such a question yet I never said it. He started telling me that he was gay and all those stuff. I told him it was not a biggie for me and that was his sexuality and I wont be mad at someone who helped and showed me good heart unless I was a fool. He asked me whether I was interested in having any girl or boy for the night he could arrange some. I told him I was not into such stuff and I was tired. I also told him that it was good for him to be what he feels and do what he wants but being Just was the best way of being human. He told me that he only gets affair with the boy I saw only and that was the reason he always makes reservations in the particular hotel. I told him it was okay and I was not going to do anything to him but I was just showing him that me helping me and his sexuality were not on the same page hence I will never be angry at his actions because it was him and I was glad that he never pretended just because of me. After that I told him I was tire and needed to sleep. He told me it was glad meeting a foreigner like me. I told him I was more glad than him and I slept in the nice scented confy bed with high wool covers and crystal while sheets. Before I could go to the dream land, I saw Neil open the door and talk to the same boy again and the two were whispering so low that I could not even pick any single word from what they said to each other. I said to myself that it was not my business and I was just a person who was helped and I should not be the burden to anyone else. after some time the door closed and the last thing I heard was an electronic lock sounding.

Bye, Bye Germany.

In the morning, I woke up before Neil because he had slept late which I was sure, I took shower and wore my clothes. I then slopped down the lobby where breakfast was served at a price. I met the room service boy I wanted to talk to yesterday and he asked whether I made him feel not safe because I never called him yesterday night and I told him, I was not part of the people he knew and I was just asking him about some thing small but I was sorry to have asked things beyond my reach. He said that he was sorry too and asked me to help me bring my breakfast to my room. I told him it was fine and I went to my room. I reached and once Neil heard me opening the door he work up and I told him he should get more sleep because he slept late. He said he was having to meet his friends at 10 AM and yet it was eight thirty in the morning. He stood up and rapped himself with the bathing stuff. Soon the room service boy came in with breakfast and I told him to put it on the table. Immediately Neil told him not to wait, but just to leave and he told him we were thankful for his services. He also got into his trouser and gave him 10e tip and the boy went off. I asked him why would he do that and he told me most boys here serve masters in some other way for tips and I was not the type of master to be served. I went a head with my breakfast and Neil finished with his bath. After some time I prepared for airport and my flight to Warsaw was at 12 noon and I had three hours. I had to check out and then we went together with Neil at the bus station and he told me I was to take another train to the airport after the stop where the bus will put the two of us. I was okay with it. We boarded the bus and after about 10 minutes we went off and Neil went with me at the train station and showed me the train to take, helped me purchase the ticket and then he hugged me and said goodbye. I waved at him and told him he was a very good person and I will not forget his hospitality. In about 20 minutes, the train had arrived and I boarded, the good thing was the train was heading to the airport direct and through. I was seated and the officer came in to check the ticket I showed mine and I was good to go. After a few minutes we had reached the station to the airport. I went off the train and stood besides the rails. I looked at the airport and was so sad that I was gonna leave the beautiful country "Germany" and all the moments, memories and enjoyments I had. I literally cried from my heart and I went to the airport check in. I went to the security check and the queue was so long and non-selective. I had to endure and stand in the line. The good thing was the security passages were more than ten and taking less than a minute for each person thus in about thirty minutes I was through with the security check in. I hurried to reach the flight check in and since the airport was so big, I moved and got tired in the process till when I finally reached. The check in toll had not been started functioning and no one was at the gate "Officials" but traveller were many. We queued and waited for the next thirty minutes and the of ficials arrived and started to work on us. One by one we slowly got finished and I was among the last group. We then were sent to the flight boarding gate 74 which was very far. My flight to Warsaw was a local flight with in Europe and so it was less flight time. Before I reached the gate, I passed via the tourist shop with duty free items and bought some souvenirs for me and some special people. On reaching the gate 74, it was about 10 minutes to boarding time and I saw a black dude who was sitting alone and most chairs were occupied, I decided to sit with him and soon as I sat, he looked at me and I greeted him. He replied and we all kept quiet. After some time he told me his name, "I am Alpha" and I also told him mine and he said he was from South Africa and I told him mine nationality. Just after a few minutes, boarding was started and we boarded for Warsaw. because it was so freeing for me I was wearing long sleeved shirt overlapping my hands. Luckily we sat on the seats next to each other. He asked me questions and I was answering, I then asked him why he was staying in Warsaw and he told me he does his business there and he had just come for a meeting in Berlin. I was surprised and I asked him the type of business he was into and he told me he was into gas and energy. we never talk for long because the flight was just one hour.

Back to Default

Once the flight from Berlin to Warsaw was done, I passed through and followed the transiting passenger, I had to look for the passport control center and I was having less time because the lay over was less than two hours. I reached to the officer and asked him where I would find the passport control and he led me to the place. I met a long queue of people, and many were from USA and the ladies behind me were talking about me. I looked behind and they told me they were talking about my outfit and they liked it. I went to the passport control and I was granted exit. I hurried to reach the gate I was to get my flight. On reaching the gate, I got to know that 90% of the passengers were Indians and because I was heading to Mumbai, it showed me that many Indians were having life in Europe. I sat just next to a man who seemed to be non-Indian and he asked me where I was heading and once I told him India, he was surprised and asked me whether I was student or worker. I told him I was student and he told me he was a cultural book writer and he was heading to India to study about the culture and morals of India specifically in Southern part. I was surprised and he asked me the part I was heading too, when I told him it was the southern part he told me it would be great if we meet again in India after the flights. I told him I would also like it but I was a student who is highly monitored and it was not easy to meet once I entered school but all is possible. The boarding time was announced and we started boarding in ranks from First class, Premium, business, premium economy to economy.

Warsaw to Mumbai.

On board, we were told to have our seats as indicated by the boarding pass. The attendants told us to strictly only touch our luggage and those who are not able to upload their luggage will be helped by the nearby attendants. As you know large planes, tri-seating, I sat with an India electrical engineer who was heading to India (back home) for vacation and no third person in our row. We sat and got confy when he asked me where I was going in India exactly. I told him in the south basically Andhra Pradesh. I asked him what he does in Poland and he told me he was an employee in Poland in an electrical company, I asked him many things like how he got the opportunity, what he studied and till which level and he finally gave me his contact and told me to keep in sync. In less than 20 minutes, we started our ascend to the sky and since it was about to be dark, the process created a beautiful view and the man next to me started recording the ascend with all its glancing and eye catching views of the horizon and the majestic city of Warsaw. After the ascend and we had obtained stability in altitude, the attendants gave us earphones of which I went with mine till my college. As usual movies, music and other stuff like games and map showing the travel process are the major forms of entertainment in the plane.I shifted my seat to sleep mode and loaded the movie called "Shang Chi, the legend of ten rings". the travel or flight time was approximately seven and half hours and the movie was less than two hours. I watched and during the first one hour, the served us with drinks and I took seven cups of mango juice with a few cups of water. As we were making about two hours of flight dinner was served, and again drinks. Since I had flown with the same flying company I knew the policy and I just kept on asking for refills in my glasses for the drinks because I was not having sleep at all. Finally I slept for about four hours and left the movie playing. Waking up was my neighbour who was in need of way through to the toilet. Once I woke up we were having less than three hours to flight end and I requested for some more water. In about 30 minutes, we were served with breakfast. I took few cups of coffee and water. The cleaning towels they gave us were beautifully scented and I had to take some in my bag to keep the memory and also use some at the hotel where I was to make reservation before my flight to Visakhapatnam. After about two hours, the captain announced for our descend and seat belts were to be tied. We descended harmoniously and reaching India (Mumbai) at around 4 AM in the morning. On landing we all headed to the passport control "Emigration" and reaching this place were many people and the entry forms were over and we had to wait. I was very tired and wanted to sleep. I waited and stood in the queue for about one hour when I got to get my entry stamp. I headed for baggage claim and got my bag, passed via the forex-station and exchanged all the Euros I had to Indian rupees. I headed out, and on the exit I met some two men and on of them wanted to scum me. He asked me whether I never had drugs in my luggage and I was surprised because asking me such a question at the exit was strange. I told him that I was clean and he was free to check my luggage in front of an officer. I then called an officer who was patrolling around and asked him to help me. As the man saw I was calling an officer, he told me to pass through the exit and go. The officer then came and got hold of outside and asked me why I was calling him. I told him about the man and he told me to show him the person. When I looked around I saw the man walking towards the end of the terminal and I told officer who whistled and the man was told to stop. They got hold of him and asked him why was he claiming duties he was not to do. Then I told the officer that I had a flight to catch in one hour at terminal 2 thus I needed to go. The officers agreed to let me go after checking my documents and my luggage again. I went and left the imposter man in the hands of the officer. I sloped down and found officers and asked them I was in need of a place to rest till my flight at 2 PM. The officer handed me over to a man who drove me to the nearby accommodation which was really expensive and I thought to get the best services. I had been in Mumbai accommodations but when I tried booking, they had all full reservations and the others were very far from the airport.

Money wasted.

The Auto-driver dropped me to an accommodation which was so basic and I expected it to be cheap, the owner charged me highly and yet I was to stay for less than 12 hours. I paid in vain, but I had hope that the place had good services like good rooms, bathroom and other extra-services. I was led to my room and I even broke down. The room was small, and dirty. This first impression killed my moods and my appetite to stay. I had already paid my money and had no other choice but to stay for the desired time and them leave for my flight in the afternoon. I looked at the towel provided in the room, it was dirty (a white towel looking creamish with dark brown patches at the center). Looking at the bed, it was dirty and smelling. No internet connection. I was doomed. I decided to take a shower and I opened my bag, got hold of my towel and soap, reaching the bathroom. I saw dirty toilets, showering can and even human hair was still hanging in the conner of the showerroom. I was so disappointed and due to this I took a shower in the most scared way. It was very hot in in Mumbai and after showering within ten minutes I was in need of air conditioner. I went a head and switched it on, to my surprise it was not working but oozing out dirty watery fluids which were so disgusting and I had to switch it off. I then has to switch on the fan, the fan was so noisy that it was hard to sleep and more so the bed in the room scared me at first with the dirty sheets and blanket I never stepped on it even at once. I decide to open my laptop and do some other work as well as check my emails. Once I opened the WiFi, I was surprised that based on the whole amount I paid, the WiFi was not working at all and when I went to the reception to complain, the people at the reception by that time, none knew English and the person I met at the time of arrival had gone. Painfully I had to stay in this room till two in the afternoon for my flight. I slept at the chair covering myself my towel. After about six hours of sleep, I woke up and went outside to get brunch, because I had slept at almost morning time, I never took breakfast and I woke up a few hours to lunch time. I moved around the area looking for a good restaurant but it seemed I was in the deep village part of Mumbai. The place was having non pleasant un-natural smell coupled with automobile pollution, muddy with many stray animals I was in fear of buying anything or even eating anything at all. The first shop I found, I asked for a soft drink and once they gave me I immediately opened it because I was hungry, it was having un-usual colouration on the drinking part, I looked at the expiry date and it was expired. I told the shopkeeper that why would he sale expired goods and he gave me another one which was the same story. He then handed me back my money and I looked for another shop and got the soft-drink and at the same shop I bought two packed biscuits and went back to my horror room. After a few hours, I left for the airport, reaching I had not made mandatory online check in, I met an operative for the flying company I was to use and she helped me do the check in as well as get the baggage tags and she directed me to the next step. I hurried because my flight was less then 30 minutes to departure. Reaching the final security check point, I was surprised because the queue was so long that I was to stay at in line for more than 30 minutes. I then saw an officer passing by and told him my flight was in 20 minutes and I requested him to pass me through very fast because I would miss my flight. He then got hold of my hand and took me to the front and I was saved by the good hearted officer. On reaching the gate I was among the last people to enter, I boarded for my last flight to the city of destiny (Visakhapatnam).

At last, I was back to College.

Reaching Visakhapatnam I went out of the airport and looked at both sides with no one holding my name or even calling it. But I was used to such come backs and I just rolled my luggage to the pick up point where cubs and taxis are always on waiting. I ordered one using the online application and in about few minutes, it arrived to my pick up. I entered and told the driver that I was going to such a University and he basically charged me extra claiming that the online-application charged less than the actual amount. I was just tire and wanted to reach back to my university and hostel to have shower and sleep. We agreed on a small increment in the amount and he started the journey. In about one hour, we had reached and I told the driver to reach me at the hostel entrance. When I reached, I got no one to welcome me and even those who saw me by-passed me like saw no one. Of-course I was used to such behaviour and it was all nothing to me. Luckily when I reached the reception, I was welcomed by the guards and went to the warden to report my coming back then handed back my room key. The journey of 1000 miles had become no more and the only things left were stories to tell.

End

We all move, travel, and even go to the wild for adventuring but the best of us are those who share their experiences with those who want to hear them. Living and exploring are the fundamentals of learning, and learning will never end for all living beings. K.Idrisa.